A Mennonite Polity
for Ministerial Leadership

Sponsored by
Mennonite Board of Congregational Ministries
Elkhart, Indiana

Ministerial Leadership Services
and the General Board of the
General Conference Mennonite Church
Newton, Kansas

Everett J. Thomas, Editor

FAITH & LIFE
P R E S S

Newton, Kansas • Winnipeg, Manitoba

Library of Congress Number 96-84443

International Standard Book Number 0-87303-319-1

Printed in the United States of America.

Introduction

From 1987 to 1995, a group of pastors and church agency administrators discussed, debated, and eventually agreed on a proposed polity for ministerial leadership in the General Conference Mennonite Church and the Mennonite Church. Motivation for this conversation derived from the possible integration of the two denominations in 1995. It has been our committee's hope that a joint GC/MC ministerial leadership polity document will contribute to the unity of an integrated Mennonite denomination in North America.

Do we speak of "leadership ministries" or "ministerial leadership"? Is an elder the same in both Mennonite traditions? And, perhaps most importantly, will both traditions accept a new protocol that calls for sharing leadership authority in the congregation among three different kinds of ministerial leaders: the pastor, the representative from the area conference, and the primary lay leader(s) in the congregation?

The General Conference Mennonite Church funded this project through the General Board. Mennonite

Church funding has been provided by the Mennonite Board of Congregational Ministries (MBCM). After eight years of meetings, this document represents our consensus. We offer it to both denominations as a way to set directions for the future. While we have laid out a particular order, it is appropriate to read this document in any order.

Finally, we acknowledge the contributions made to this project by five persons not on the final committee: Harold Bauman, John Neufeld, Paul Zehr, and Gordon Zook served on the committee at various times during these years. Ralph Lebold was the primary writer for the Mennonite Church history section.

Willis L. Breckbill, *Co-chair*   Doris Gascho
Brenda Martin Hurst, *Co-chair*   Michael A. Meneses
Bill Block   Erick Sawatzky
John P. Braun   Dale Stoltzfus
John A. Esau   Everett J. Thomas

January 1996

Preface

For some time, area conferences in the Mennonite Church and the General Conference Mennonite Church have written guidelines that assist them in their responsibilities to call, credential, and occasionally discipline ministers. A *Mennonite Polity for Ministerial Leadership* borrows heavily from these practices and seeks to offer uniformity and clarity across the church.

Mennonite congregations in North America have borrowed freely, at times, from corporate, academic, or political models for leadership. Such borrowing was often done without reflection or without determining whether the model was consistent with Anabaptist Mennonite belief and practice. For example, Mennonite congregations have increasingly assumed an "employer/employee mentality" when dealing with persons who have been called by God and the church to serve in ministry. In addition, we have moved from decision making by discernment to accepting majority rule as our model. Furthermore, lawsuits against conferences, ministers, and other church leaders are on the increase. It is apparent that we need collaborative wisdom for this time, and some correctives. Consequently, this document emerges out of reflection on our biblical and historical roots and seeks to reground our current practice of ministry.

Anticipating Integration

Beyond the cultural context in which we find ourselves, the merger of the General Conference Mennonite Church and the Mennonite Church in North America will bring Mennonite congregations with different histories and traditions into closer relationship. We will discover that Mennonite groups have very different leadership traditions and will be challenged to develop a common understanding of congregational governance. It is our hope that this document can contribute to the unity of the church for years to come by offering a ministerial leadership polity that will serve all North American congregations, be their history General Conference or Mennonite Church.

How Was This Document Tested and Refined?

This document is now in its sixth and final draft. The first draft was created and then reviewed by the ten-member Polity Committee. The second draft was reviewed by the General Conference and Mennonite Church conference ministers in their annual meeting in Kitchener, Ontario, in May 1994. Their counsel shaped the third draft, which was subsequently tested with a group of seventy "readers" in the fall of 1994. This group included Mennonite theologians, pastors, bishops, conference staff ... a great cloud of witnesses who have been immersed in ministerial issues most of their lives.

The counsel from these readers shaped a fourth draft which was reviewed in early 1995 by the Mennonite Board of Congregational Ministries, Mennonite Church General Board, and the General Conference Committee on the Ministry. Their counsel and additional Polity Committee discernment shaped a fifth draft which was examined by both General Boards (Mennonite Church and General Conference Mennonite Church). The final draft reflects changes requested by the two General Boards when they approved this document in November 1995.

What This Document Is NOT

It has been necessary to be clear about what is included and what is *not* included in this document. This is a document dealing only with the leadership structure at the center of congregational life. We have *not* attempted to speak to all congregational roles nor to all the issues germane to membership in a congregation. Because Mennonite theology expects every congregation to be a part of a larger body, the document addresses the *leadership* connection between congregation and conference. It does not, however, address the relationship of one conference to another conference. In other words, this is a document addressed to only one part of church life: the relationship of ministerial leaders to congregations, conferences, and denominations.

How to Use This Document

We believe the document points toward a more "churchly" way of being with each other. It is for guidance and counsel. It should be used to discern direction. It should not be viewed as a legalistic code; rather, it establishes a trajectory of change which each congregation and conference can follow, as is befitting to their needs and situations.

This document and the polity it describes is commended to pastors, congregational leaders, and persons with responsibility for congregational oversight, those who have responsibility for ministerial credentials and/or the call of ministers, seminaries, denominational offices, and anyone with an interest in congregational leadership structures in the General Conference and Mennonite Church.

In order to familiarize the Mennonite Church in North America with the document, we encourage conferences to set up in-service training events for elders, deacons, ministers, and overseers or bishops. We urge its discussion in churchwide gatherings and in ministerial clusters. We encourage seminaries to use it in courses or interterms.

May it provide guidance, support, counsel, and a sense of unity with each other and with Jesus Christ, our cornerstone.

Doris Gascho
Everett J. Thomas

January 1996

Table of Contents

Section V. Ethics in Ministry

Fellow laborers with me in the ministry,
  Guardians and trumpeters are they,
  Spiritual pillars are they,
  Messengers of peace are they called,
  Bishops and overseers are they called,
  Shepherds are they called,
  Teachers are they called,
  The light of the world are they called,
  The salt of the earth are they called,
  Ministers are they called in Christ's stead.
  Brothers and sisters, serve but do not lord it.

Adapted from Menno Simons

Section I.
Theological Background

A. Biblical and Theological Basis for a Mennonite Polity

Definition of "Ministry"

The term "ministry" has several meanings in the Mennonite Church and in the General Conference Mennonite Church. The term ministry in this document is intended to be understood in two ways:

- In its broadest sense, ministry denotes the service to which the whole people of God is called. This calling may be as individuals, as a local community of believers, as a congregation which is part of a conference of congregations, or as the universal church.

- In a second sense, the terms *minister*, *ministry*, or *ministries* refer to the particular institutional forms which this service may take. In Mennonite experience and tradition, these particular institutional forms may or may not be *ordained*, but they are often referred to as *offices of ministry*. (See the Glossary for definitions of terms used in this document.)

Ministry is rooted in God's reconciling and saving work in the world. Initially, God sought to reconcile and heal a broken world by calling a people to live in a covenant relationship of obedience and transformation. As the people of God, Israel was to be a witness for God in the world so that through her all "families of the earth might be blessed" (Gen. 12:3). The love, grace, and justice of God was revealed through such acts as the deliverance of Israel from slavery in Egypt; the making of covenant and the giving of the Ten Commandments; the provision of political, social, and spiritual leadership; and the growth and disciplining of the nation.

Then God spoke in a unique and decisive way in Jesus:

Jesus came into Galilee, preaching the gospel of God, and saying, "The time is fulfilled, and the kingdom of God is at hand; repent, and believe in the gospel" (Mk. 1:14-15, RSV).

Jesus' ministry was concerned with the kingdom, a community shaped by the reign of God. Jesus proclaimed and modeled such a community, even by his death on the cross. Through Jesus, persons experienced life in God's reign, expressed love and praise to God, served their neighbors, and lived a life of mutual love, forgiveness, reconciliation, and self-sacrifice. All true Christian ministry must convey this message of reconciliation and service.

All Christian ministry is grounded in a theology of the church. From the beginning, it has been the will of God to be in fellowship with humankind and for humans to live in harmony with one another. God elected a people to be a light to the nations. The church is a visible presence of God's ongoing work around the globe, a worshiping and serving community initiated by Jesus, God's son, and empowered by the Holy Spirit. Through the act of baptism, believers covenant to be members of one another in this new body of Christ and to live a new life of holiness and service in accordance with the spiritual gifts given to them.

The corporate, historical, and ethnic dimensions of the body of Christ and the accompanying expressions of holiness, service, fellowship, and communion take place in the context of the social and cultural dimensions of human experience. Discipline, structure, and organization consistent with the Gospel of Christ are, therefore, required to equip the church for ministry. However, all pastoral and caregiving ministries are grounded in God's grace.

Mennonite ministry finds its basis in New Testament. New Testament images, concepts, and practices usually have historical roots in the Old Testament. So it is also with ministry. Hebrew and Greek language for ministry in the Old Testament distinguishes between the kind of service in worship (*latruein*) and inner service (*douleuein*): *inner service* to God shows itself through mercy, justice, and righteousness. The priests of the sanctuary who come near to minister to Yahweh as well as non-priestly persons like Joshua and Elisha characterize the two realities. Further, in the Jewish community, elders were routinely chosen and appointed from the wiser and more experienced members to provide counsel, make decisions for the community, interpret doctrines, and discipline offenders.

The tradition of inner calling of service to God finds its way into the New Testament more strongly than the tradition of the priests in worship. Jesus quoted Hosea: "I desire mercy, and not sacrifice" (Mt. 9:13, RSV) and to the Samaritan woman he said, "A time is coming and has now come when the true worshipers will worship the Father in spirit and truth..." (Jn. 4:23, NIV). Paul, in Romans 12:1; 14:18; and 1 Thessalonians 1:9, picks up the inner service theme and amplifies it. It is not the "set-apart" serving of the priest and Levite which is stressed as much as the everyday faithful service of all God's people, even as various offices of ministry are discussed.

The language and array of images in the New Testament regarding ministry are both varied and complex. Literally dozens of words and images are used to describe the multifaceted dimensions of ministry. Of these *diakonos* (servant, deacon), *apostolos* (apostle), *presbuteros* (elder, presbyter), *episcopos* (overseer, bishop), *evangelistas* (evangelist), and *poimen* (pastor, shepherd) are most common to us. These persons shared in the ministry of the early church, both gathered and scattered.

In addition to special terms and images, several New Testament passages speak directly about ministry. In Ephesians 4:1-16, 1 Corinthians 12-14, and Romans 12, special emphasis is given to the nature and place of spiritual gifts, to the primacy of love, the body of Christ imagery, and the role of ministry in promoting healthy body life. Humility, self-sacrifice, and hospitality are stressed as essential qualities of faithful ministry. First Peter 4:10-11 stresses service and grounding in God. Chapter 5:1-4 views Jesus Christ as the "Chief Shepherd" and calls the elders to be shepherds of God's flock. Second Corinthians is devoted almost entirely to ministry themes. Paul defends and discusses his calling as an apostle, his response to opposition, and puts forth such metaphors for ministry as "the aroma of Christ," "ambassador," and "agents of reconciliation." In addition to these passages, we also look to the actual ministry of the early church as in Acts and the epistles.

It is in the earthly ministry of Jesus that we find particular reference and meaning. Jesus' ministry derived from his relationship with God, which resulted in the certainty of his call and "sentness." In Jesus we see one who "made himself nothing, taking the very nature of a servant" (Phil. 2:7, NIV), being obedient to God, even unto death, yet ministering with authority, confidence, compassion, and competence. We see Jesus' ministry:

1. Finding its locus and authority in God (Mk. 1:35)
2. Being responsible to God (Lk. 4:1-13)
3. Proclaiming the Kingdom of God (Lk. 4:18-19)
4. Instructing in the way of God (Mt. 5—7)
5. Confronting evil powers and deliverance (Lk. 11:14-20)
6. Demonstrating compassion (Mk. 1:29-34)
7. Celebrating life (Jn. 2:1-11)
8. Walking in prayerful relationship with God (Jn. 5:16-27)
9. Calling persons to a response of commitment and discipleship (Jn. 3:1-21)
10. Respecting the freedom of others (Lk. 18:18-25)
11. Practicing "revolutionary subordination" (Mt. 26:57-67)
12. Empowering others for ministry (Mt. 16:17-19)
13. Selecting twelve to carry on a specific ministry.

Clearly, Jesus' way of ministry and leadership was to be powerful yet not domineering, authoritative but not authoritarian, life-giving and liberating, and loving even unto death. Likewise, Jesus sought to equip those whom he sent out with similar characteristics (Mk. 3:14-15). He taught his followers that "the greatest among you become as the youngest, and the leader as one who serves" (Lk. 22:26, RSV). He also taught them to go in the name of Christ (Mt. 28:19-20) and in the power of the Spirit (Acts 1:8) to minister with authority (Mt. 18:15-20).

From such studies come the convictions that:

1. Christian ministry is given to the gathered people of God (*laos*).
2. Jesus' life and ministry directs our lives and ministries in a special and particular way.
3. Christian ministry is the living Christ doing God's work through a faithful people empowered by the Holy Spirit.
4. The forms of Christian ministry are richly varied and diverse, yet are related in that they derive from the same Spirit and are interdependent because the church is essentially the one body of Christ.

A Mennonite understanding of ministry affirms the ministry of all baptized believers. Jesus called his followers to active discipleship. He gave them a commission to "go and make disciples of all nations, baptizing them ... and teaching them" (Mt. 28:19-20, NIV). The early church recognized that the call to conversion and discipleship involved the call to ministry, mission, and evangelism. According to Ephesians 4:8, Christ's saving work and his present rule as Lord includes distributing gifts to each in the church. The description of the whole body working properly, of becoming mature, and of reaching the fullness of Christ is applied to the many and shared ministries working together in the church. This same pattern is described as the work of the Holy Spirit in 1 Corinthians 12 and as participating in the body of Christ in Romans 12.

A Mennonite understanding of ministry affirms calling out persons to offices of ministry. All members of the body of Christ are bestowed with ministering gifts, and the word *ministry* can be rightfully used in reference to the service to which the gathered people of God (*laos*) is called. However, we also affirm some members are called to a variety of ministerial *offices*. The many references in Mennonite Confessions of Faith and the numerous references in the New Testament to "elders," "deacons," "overseers," "bishops," "shepherds," or "pastors" are evidence of the need for ministerial offices. The concept of ministerial office in the believers church tradition refers to those roles and functions:

1. Through which other members are better equipped to participate in the church's ministry,
2. To which persons are called and appointed on a continuing and long-term basis,
3. Which are representative of a local congregation or the church body as a whole,
4. Which carry a particular responsibility for community leadership and oversight.

Persons who fill a ministerial leadership office thus include but are not necessarily limited to pastors, teachers, elders, lay leaders, evangelists, missionaries, pastoral counselors, chaplains, overseers, bishops, and church administrators.

Since the offices of ministerial leadership belong to the church, not the individual, it is the church's responsibility to discern and identify members' gifts and character and to help them understand how they can best contribute to the ministry of God's people. This includes helping persons to learn how to live and minister in community, to ascertain the most appropriate way and place in which their gifts should be deployed, and to decide whether to enter or to continue in ministerial office. Such decisions should be made in prayer and in conversation with others in the Christian community.

As a church committed to God's vision of reconciling all persons in Christ and breaking down all dividing walls of hostility (Eph. 2), we affirm that God bestows ministry gifts and God calls persons to leadership ministries without regard to gender, race, ethnic/cultural origin, or social standing. We, as the community of God's people, call out persons in the same manner. We believe there is, therefore, no place in Mennonite ministry for discrimination on the basis of gender, race, social standing, or ethnic/cultural origin. The elements of all members being called to an identifiable ministry, of the diversity and variety of ministries, and of sharing in particular ministries are thus rooted in the work of Christ and the Holy Spirit.

Ministry takes on richly varied and diverse forms. The New Testament does not offer one fixed form of leadership in the early church or for all times and places. What the New Testament refers to as elders, deacons, bishops, and pastors come closest to what we mean today when we speak of leadership or ministry in the congregation. These leadership offices help the congregation find overall direction and enable the many gifts and ministries to work together in the church as well as in the church's mission in the world. Even though these ministry offices are needed in the congregation, New Testament descriptions show that there were other types of leaders/ministers in the broader church and in the local congregation. Teachers, apostles, missionaries, and evangelists are examples.

As in the New Testament church, the Mennonite Church in North America today does not reflect one uniform model of ministerial leadership. The rich diversity of leadership forms reflects the gifts of the Holy Spirit and the richness of Christ's lordship. For Mennonites in North America, this diversity is compounded by our members becoming increasingly urbanized, professional, and influenced by contemporary culture. With such changes and cultural accommodation comes an increasing variety of ministerial roles, both within the church and outside the church. In hospitals, mental health centers, special care facilities, and prisons, people express the need and desire for the gospel of Christ, spiritual care, and loving community. *Chaplains* provide such a ministry.

This document intends to point toward common understandings of ministry which will embrace this diversity of ministering roles. To both unify our understanding yet embrace the diversity which exists, this document calls for an understanding of ministry in the church which embraces a threefold pattern:

1. The ministry which provides oversight to the church: to conferences, congregations, and pastors (e.g., conference ministers, overseers, and bishops).
2. The ministry which provides prophetic, priestly, and administrative service in a local and/or specific setting (e.g., pastors, missionaries, chaplains, teachers).
3. The ministry which represents the members of the congregation and shares responsibility to lead a congregation with the previous two offices (e.g., elders/deacons, lay ministers).

Such a model allows for order, diversity, and creativity. It expects authority to be both corporate and individual. It expresses services to one another rather than lording it over others. It is marked by mutual accountability and personal responsibility for all persons in ministerial leadership with each other and before the Lord of the church.

Mennonite ministry proclaims the gospel of Christ. Having affirmed the various and diverse forms of ministry in a pluralistic society, we nevertheless affirm only one central message—Jesus Christ. The centrality of ministry is not found in managing plurality or mediating between cultural realities. Rather, the centrality of ministry is the message of Christ. The Mennonite minister's central concern is to know God and to proclaim God's Word to all the world—in the church and outside it. The minister's life is, therefore, a life of study, prayer, contemplation, and action in and on the Word of God, God's creation, the lives of people, and the events of life in the world. Through the inexhaustibility of God's love and power, the richness of God's creation, and the unlimited surprises of people, ministry finds its center.

Ministry receives its authority both from God and the church. The authority for ministry in the New Testament is rooted in Jesus Christ, who received it from God and who conferred it upon those in ministry by the Holy Spirit in the church. We too affirm the empowering call from God through Christ as essential for authoritative ministry. We also recognize the mediating role of the church in discerning the minister's call and blessing it. Individual gifts, training, and quality of service are all involved. Hence, the church and its leaders must be accountable both to God and to each other as they respond to the call of ministry and the exercising of authority.

To speak of the source of authority and dual accountability does not yet address the question of what does authority consist? Authority for ministry consists of at least three related but separate realities: *task*, *office*, and *being*.

Task is perhaps the easiest to define because it is the most visible aspect of ministry. The woman or man in ministry performs such tasks as preaching, teaching, visitation, administration, and admonition. A degree of authority is invested in the performance of these tasks.

Office is a symbolic way of speaking about the representational role that a minister fulfills on behalf of the church. Authority for fulfilling these roles is accorded to the position, not the person. When the church ordains, licenses, or commissions, it installs a person into a position which already is endowed with authority.

The *being* dimension of ministry adds a third layer of complexity which addresses the spiritual, emotional, and relational core of the minister. By demonstrating spiritual depth and maturing in the context of competent ministry, the minister earns what has been conferred by the church earlier through ordination, licensing, or commissioning.

Finally, the exercise of authority is to be in the name and spirit of Jesus and the New Testament Scriptures, "speaking the truth in love" and not "lording it over others." Having been given authority, ministers are to build the body of Christ and seek the will of God together with other members for the mutual strengthening and health of all.

B. Understanding Ordination

Ordination is a rite of the church which confirms those whom God and the church have called to particular roles of ministerial leadership in and for the church.

Its roots go back to the Old Testament and instructions given to Moses to consecrate Aaron and his sons as priests for the congregation of God's people (Ex. 29 and Lv. 8, 9, and 10). Over a period of seven days, Israelites observed a prescribed series of washings, clothings, anointings, sacrifices, meals, and offerings until in the end, "Aaron lifted his hands toward the people and blessed them ..., and the glory of the LORD appeared to all the people" (Lv. 9:22-23, NIV).

Although there is no clear mandate for such a ceremony in the New Testament, there are numerous examples of Jesus and the church lending their blessing and confirmation to persons called and sent to represent God and the church in service and witness. (Luke 9:1-6, the mission of the twelve; Matthew 28:16-20, the commissioning of the disciples; John 21:15-19, Jesus' words to Peter; Acts 6:1-7, Seven chosen to serve; Acts 13:1-3, Barnabas and Saul commissioned; Acts 1:12-26, Matthias chosen to replace Judas; 2 Timothy 1:6, Timothy—the laying on of hands.)

It was not until the third century A.D. that ordination to ministerial leadership is described and defined as a specific rite of the church in response to the biblical mandate that "all things should be done decently and in order" (1 Cor. 14:40, RSV).

Schisms and heresies in the early Christian church revealed the need to order leadership so as to protect, maintain, and defend the apostolic faith. Following the advice to Timothy, "Do not ordain anyone hastily" (1 Tim. 5:22a, NRSV), the church found it necessary to lend clarity to leadership roles and relationships within the community of faith.

In the Anabaptist confessions of the sixteenth and seventeenth centuries, there is little specific guidance as to either the meaning or the practice of ordination, yet the ceremony is assumed and spoken of in the following manner: "But if the shepherd should be driven away or led to the Lord by the cross, at the same hour another shall be ordained (verordnet) to his place,..." (Schleitheim 1527). "Also that the apostles were afterwards, as faithful followers of Christ and leaders of the church, diligent in these matters, namely, in choosing through prayer and supplication to God, brethren who were to provide all the churches in the cities and circuits, with bishops, pastors, and leaders, and to ordain to these offices such men as took heed unto themselves and unto the doctrine,..." (Dordrecht 1632).

In a similar vein, the Ris Confession speaks about ministers of the church being "solemnly installed in their office provided they accept the call and have first been examined and proved" (Ris Confession 1766-1895).

What Is Ordination?

Ordination is an act of the church (congregation, conference, and denomination) which calls and appoints a member to ongoing leadership ministry in the life and mission of the church (see Glossary). The ordination rite includes the covenant between the church and the minister being ordained, the laying on of hands, and the prayer of ordination. When the church ordains a man or woman to ministerial leadership, it intends to say at least the following:

1. We confirm the call of God to the person being ordained for ministry within or on behalf of the church. It is a time of blessing and celebration by the church for the gracious gifts of God to all, inasmuch as the ordained ministry is part of the ministry of the whole church.

2. We affirm the person for the unique leadership gifts the minister brings to the Christian community. We recognize the investment in spiritual, relational, and intellectual growth through completion of special training for this role within the church. We affirm a clarity of identity as shepherds of the church and servants of Jesus Christ.

3. We identify the person being ordained as one who in some way represents God in a "priestly" role

within the community of faith where all are priests serving God (Rv. 1:6; 5:10). As such, we recognize the role of spiritual leadership within the church, a leadership growing out of an authentic humanity, and an authentic spirituality disciplined by a life of prayer, contemplation, and the Scriptures.

4. We entrust an office of ministry to the person being ordained. By this, we empower this person to act in a representative way on the church's behalf with both the privileges and the responsibilities of this office. Within this ministerial office, we recognize an authority which is granted for leadership within the church. Paradoxically, this authority must constantly be earned by evidence of wisdom, competence, integrity, humility, and perception.

5. We call the person being ordained to particular tasks associated with this office: to preach and teach; to lead with vision and wisdom; to equip members to release their spiritual gifts; to provide pastoral care; to be responsible for the church's rites of marriage, baptism, observance of the Lord's table; and to help represent the church in the local community and in the conference of congregations.

6. We covenant between the congregation and the person ordained a mutual accountability of support, respect, and care. For the person ordained, accountability to the church includes at least the following: personal moral integrity, faithfulness as stewards of the gospel, living example of equality and servanthood in relation to others, and effectiveness in exercising this ministry. The congregation covenants to pray for the ordained person, to give

and receive counsel, to support his/her leadership ministry, and respect the authority of the office into which the minister has been ordained.

7. We declare our trust in the person being ordained by providing a *credential* for leadership ministry; the credential is primarily for service within the church, and, secondly, a credential also acknowledged in society and by the state.

Who Is to Be Ordained?

The call to ministry is in the context of one's new birth into a living and abiding relationship with God through Christ. Ministerial leadership presumes that a person is committed to Christ and the church through baptism, has a membership covenant with a Mennonite congregation, and subscribes to the current Mennonite Confession of Faith. When the church ordains members for particular leadership offices, the church confirms:

- those who reflect the biblical standards of Christian living such as in the fruits of the spirit: "love, joy, peace, patience, kindness, generosity, faithfulness, gentleness, and self-control" (Gal. 5:22-23).

- those who believe that servanthood is taught by Jesus as the central defining characteristic of all true leaders and strive to live it in their lives (Mk. 10:42-45).

- those whose lives model the biblical expectations of leadership for pastors, bishops, deacons, and elders (1 and 2 Cor.; 1 and 2 Tm.; Ti.; 1 Pt. 5:1-11).

- those called to special tasks and ministries in and for the church (Rom. 12:6-8; 1 Cor. 12; Eph. 4:11-13).

Ordination is appropriate for persons in pastoral ministries in the congregation, as well as ministries in specialized settings (chaplains, pastoral counselors, administrators of church institutions), provided that their primary service is to and/or for the church in priestly and prophetic roles. Ordination is not necessarily applicable or appropriate, however, just because a person is employed by an institution owned by or related to the church.

Ordination is appropriate also for persons in missionary service, again assuming that their primary service is in ministries such as evangelism, church planting, pastoring, or chaplaincy.

Affirming that in Christ "there is no longer Jew or Greek, there is no longer slave or free, there is no longer male and female; for all of you are one in Christ Jesus" (Gal. 3:28, NRSV), cultural/ethnic origin, race, class, and gender are not criteria for determining who is acceptable for ordination.

Affirming also the mercy and forgiveness of God, few sinful acts would permanently disqualify a person from ordination and ministry. An ordained person should give ample evidence in life and attitude to stand before the church as an example of God's redeeming love at work. (See also Section IV, "Qualifications for Ministry")

Who Ordains?

While the ultimate meaning of ordination rests in the gifts and graces which God provides and ordains, we still must ask from a human point of view *who* it is that ordains. The *church* ordains those whom it calls to the office of ministry.

But what do we mean by the church? We mean to include the church as the congregation in a specific place and time, the congregation of which the person being ordained is a member and in whose presence this person is called to serve. But we also mean the church in its larger sense of the regional gathering of congregations in area conferences as well as the whole church as represented by the denomination.

In the processes and acts of ordination, the several elements of the church (congregation, conference, denomination) are called upon to exercise discrete roles of discernment and affirmation. The person to be ordained is, in turn, accountable not only to the congregation but also to the conference which grants the ministerial credential and to the Mennonite denomination to which the conference belongs.

While it is the church which ordains, a previously ordained person(s) leads the ordination ceremony. While the Mennonite church is not committed to a formal tradition of apostolic succession, we nevertheless recognize that those ordained by the church have a particular task of preserving and propagating the apostolic faith. Orderly transmission of the ordained ministry is a powerful symbol of the continuity of the church and its faith through history. Therefore, it is expected that an ordained person or persons will lead in the ordination ceremony. This should include a conference minister or someone to represent the larger church; often all ordained persons present are invited to stand with the candidate during the ordination prayer. It is also appropriate to invite unordained members to stand with the candidate during the rite.

Implications of Ordination

We have not understood ordination as a "sacrament," which somehow effects an internal change or which gives to the person greater worth than any others within the Christian community. However, we recognize that insofar as we are always affected by and changed by covenant experiences, ordination may become a life-shaping and identity-giving moment. A leader so ordained is empowered to act and speak on behalf of the church in many settings. Although accountable to the church for the way in which he/she holds the privilege, an ordained minister is granted authority to represent the church both within and without the community of faith.

Ordination does have to do with offering a place or a position from which the minister seeks to fulfill his/her calling. It is not a higher or holier status, but a place from which to live and work for the church.

Traditionally, it has been understood that ordination is for life and is not, therefore, a repeatable act. Ordained persons who reach retirement age and discontinue active ministry retain both their ordination and the authorization to exercise the privileges and responsibilities granted by ordination. However, such persons exercise the privileges with accountability to the area conference, and in consultation with their own pastor and congregation.

Ordination credentials are vested in the area conference and transfer from one ministerial assignment to another within that area conference. An installation service is always an appropriate time and place for the reaffirmation of the person's ordination. *Accountability* for the credential is the responsibility of the area conference where the person resides or holds church membership.

Leadership for the ordination process is the responsibility of the area conference ministerial leadership committee. This is to be done with the discernment and support of the congregation of which the candidate is a member. Where cases of discipline and removal of credentials occur, the process is the responsibility of the area conference ministerial leadership committee in consultation with the congregation and denomination. The area conference also provides an appeal process, whereby conference actions on credentials are reviewed according to guidelines adopted for discipline in the denomination.

In very rare cases and for reasons of discipline, the church discerns if it must take action to remove credentials or to silence an ordained person. Such an action is understood as a revocation of the ordination, and the person is to be considered as no longer ordained.

Understanding Ordination

The offices of ministry are a great treasure of the church. Through careful and prayerful discernment, the church calls those to ministry whom God has chosen. By ordaining these persons to ministry, the church declares them caretakers of the gospel and shepherds of God's people. It is a sacred task; ordination is public confirmation of a minister's call to a lifetime of such service to the church.

Ministry and Mennonite History

A. Biblical and Anabaptist History

Models for Ministry and Leadership in the Old Testament

It is God, the LORD, who is the ultimate leader of the people of the covenant. It is God who first calls forth a people; it is God who delivers from slavery; it is God whose gracious love and compassion leads the community in its long journey to the land of promise; it is God who forms the nation; it is God who calls them to be priests to minister to the nations around them; and it is God who continues to forgive a less-than-perfect people while continuing to challenge them to a higher righteousness.

But this God does not work alone; this covenant-forming God calls forth those who are to be ministers and servants of the covenant. They serve both God and the people in a mediating and representative fashion. They are the priests and the levites, and they are led symbolically and truly by the high priest.

The Old Testament is not afraid of double meanings, even when speaking about something as specific as the priesthood. In its truest form, the priesthood represents something of what God intends for the whole people. "Now therefore, if you obey my voice and keep my covenant, you shall be my treasured possession out of all the peoples. Indeed, the whole earth is mine, but you shall be for me a priestly kingdom and a holy nation" (Ex. 19:5-6, NRSV). In a similar manner, we hear out of the prophetic tradition: "... you shall be called priests of the LORD, you shall be named ministers of our God;..." (Is. 61:6, NRSV).

Though serving in God's behalf, the priestly community is itself always in need of redemption. They serve, however imperfectly, in a way that responds to the deepest yearnings of God's people for salvation and shalom. Within the covenant, God provides for those who are ministers and servants in God's behalf. Though ofttimes challenged by the reforms of the prophets who also served at God's call, the priests continued throughout history to represent in an institutionalized form an essential role within the community.

It has been observed that already within the Old Testament priesthood tradition, we have the formative model for a *threefold ministry* in the high priest, the priests, and the levites. The high priest alone represents the whole of God's people; the priests serve within the sacrificial system and are the teachers and interpreters of the Law; the levites are to assist the priests and thus to serve the congregation.

In summary, "The essential function of the Levitical priesthood is therefore to assure, maintain, and constantly re-establish the holiness of the elect people of God.... Hence it is through the priesthood that a purified and sanctified Israel is able to serve God and receives his blessing" (R. Abba in *The Interpreter's Dictionary of the Bible*).

From the New Testament into Early Christian History

There is wide disagreement as to where the New Testament leaves us in regard to issues of polity in general and ministry in particular. Some claim to find clear and specific guidance in relation to these concerns; and others see the church in the New Testament as a church in the process of development, slowly moving from very loose forms toward something with quite specific but developing patterns. Erland Waltner has summarized where we are left at the end of the New Testament:

1. The organizational patterns of the government and ministry of the early church were dynamic and developmental rather than rigidly fixed. This is well illustrated in Acts 6 where organizational development came as a response to real need.

2. The Christian ministry in one sense is the function of the entire church fellowship but in its practical administration calls for Christian leadership in carrying out many and varied functions. This calls for some kind of division of labor.

3. The Christian ministry finds its true nature and authority in Jesus Christ himself rather than in the Jewish community or in the chapters of Christian history.

4. It is difficult, if not impossible, to draw sharp lines of distinction between various kinds of ministerial offices simply on the basis of the biblical text.

5. The single bishop/elder in a congregation or in a given geographical locality appears to be a historical development rather than an originally instituted pattern of church government.

6. That the practice of ordination to ministerial offices, while not prominent in the New Testament, never-

theless has a clear biblical basis, includes prayer and the laying on of hands, and has a symbolic rather than a sacerdotal significance.

At the end of the first century A.D., Ignatius is the earliest author to clearly identify a threefold ministry: the bishop, the presbytery (elders), and the deacons. The development of this ministerial structure was in large measure the response of the church to the threat of schism and/or heresy. Several centuries later, Jerome wrote:

> "That afterwards one was chosen to preside over the rest, this was done as a remedy for schism, and to prevent one individual from rending the Church of Christ by drawing it to himself ... the presbyters used always to appoint as bishop one chosen out of their number...."

We know that out of that history there developed within Christendom a ministerial hierarchy which eventually came to define the church. Ordination became one of the seven sacraments of the church, and apostolic succession defined the boundaries of who was properly ordained. With the Lutheran reformation, the church was again defined by the clergy with the preaching of the Word and the right administration of the sacraments. However, the times were right and ripe for another understanding of the church, one which would not place clergy as the defining center.

The Anabaptist Reformation

One of the strongest and most consistent emphases regarding those who would serve in ministry was that it must be God and the church who call persons to this role. Riedeman in 1542 wrote: "If the church needs one or, indeed more ministers, she must not elect them as pleases herself, but wait upon the Lord to see whom he chooses and shows them."

Menno Simons wrote in his *Foundation* document: "They were driven into this office by the Spirit of God, with pious hearts, and did ever esteem themselves unfit to serve the people of God or to execute such a high and responsible office."

It is significant that all the Anabaptist confessions, when speaking about ministry and leadership in the church, speak of an "office" of ministry as evidenced in the following excerpts:

Schleitheim 1527—"The office of such a person (Shepherds in the congregation) shall be to read and exhort and teach."

Dordrecht 1632—"Regarding the offices and elections of persons ... the church cannot exist or prosper ... without offices and regulations."

Ris Confession 1766—"Christ ... instituted various offices and conditions in His church."

Mennonite Articles of Faith, 1836—Elbing, Germany (Eblag, Poland). "We believe that the ministry in the church is a divine institution."

Articles, 1933 (never officially accepted)—"God has appointed the office of ministry in its diversified duties and departments."

Again Menno Simons uses the same language of office when he writes: "For not one can serve in this high and holy office conformable to God's will, except he whom the Lord of the vineyard has made capable by the Spirit of His grace." Certainly one of the issues which needs further interpretation for our present understanding about ministry is what these references to *office(s)* mean and how they shape our present thinking on both ministry and ordination.

Despite this emphasis on the *offices of ministry*, there was within the Anabaptist and Mennonite reformation a clear leveling of the church in the sense that ministers were no longer to be seen with a hierarchy separate from the rest of the congregation. Indeed, ministry was to be shared by everyone, for all were ministers and servants within the larger kingdom of Christ. Some were called to distinct ministry roles within the congregation.

Serving with the *Aeltester* (bishop) and the *preacher* (shepherd) was the deacon, also ordained to that office and whose special responsibility was to be a minister to the poor (*Armendiener*). In the Dordrecht confession, they were called *Almoners* (one who distributes alms) and worked alongside and with the "honorable old widows" (women in ministry roles) to "visit ... and further assist in taking care of any matters in the church that properly come within their sphere."

Over the course of time, a threefold ministry tradition again developed. By the time of the Dordrecht Confession (l632), this became quite clear: "Bishops, pastors, and leaders ... sound in the faith, pious in their life ... a good reputation ... example in all godliness and good works; might worthily administer the Lord's ordinances."

While similar understandings were developing throughout the Anabaptist reformation, differences of terminology cause confusion. In the Swiss and South German traditions, the "oversight ministry" took on the term *bishop*, while in the Dutch and North German traditions the same "oversight ministry" was referred to as *Aeltester* (a German word literally meaning "elder," but it was similar to the bishop in function). To cause even more confusion, when the oversight ministry merged with that of the preacher, the term "elder" followed and was on occasion referred to as the "Vollen-Deiner" (literally, full-service ministry).

Relatively little is said in the early Anabaptist writings about ordination; however, Krahn reports: "The Wismer Agreements (1554), ... state clearly that no one has the right to preach without being called by a congregation or ordained by an elder."

Much of our interpretation of history is selective and often conditioned out of our contemporary experience more than out of the realities of earlier centuries. Ministry is no exception. Over the course of the last generation, we have been taught to believe that the Anabaptist reformation essentially denied any differentiation between members of the church and those who were called to give ministerial leadership to the church. Such a teaching emerged from the mistaken notion that "our Anabaptist concept of the priesthood of all believers" means that every member is equally called to serve as a pastor/leader.

We now know that not only was the concept of the "priesthood of the believers more Lutheran than Anabaptist" (see *Mennonite Encyclopedia*, Vol. V) but also that from the very beginning, the Anabaptist reformation carried with it a clear and strong sense of the importance of ministerial leadership. That is not to say that ministry was not itself reformed by early Anabaptists, for it is quite clear that their reformation embodied some forms of *anti-clericalism* expressed against the

Roman church. Menno Simons, for instance, was quite prone to contrast the true and false preachers of the gospel, both by the content of their message and the manner of their lives.

What the Anabaptists rejected was the exclusive reliance upon the office of ministry without the accompanying Christian credibility of the person. The minister's faith and life were necessary and essential elements to sustain the leadership role which the church had conferred.

It is tempting to look to one's tradition to discover forms and practices which could be followed in the present time. However, we must remember that every change in ministry forms, including those of the Anabaptists, was an attempt to resolve previous failures or problems for which old forms were no longer adequate. To idealize the best of the past is often to ignore the features of the past which are no longer tenable.

Clearly, the Anabaptists stand as a continuing warning against every form of elitism among those who would be the servants of Christ and his church. Yet they demonstrated in practice that the church needs those who will exercise leadership from special offices of ministry to serve, as Menno Simons said, "in Christ's stead."

B. The Mennonite Church Story

Models and the practice of ministry in the North American (Old) Mennonite Church emerged from patterns established in South Germany, Switzerland, and France from the beginning of the movement (1525) through the late 1700s. Until the end of World War II, the "Swiss" branch of the Mennonite Church and the Amish Mennonites in North America practiced a plural or "threefold" ministry: *bishop* (sometimes called *elder*), *preacher* (occasionally called *minister*), and *deacon*. Persons were selected from within the congregation and ordained to positions of preacher, bishop, and sometimes deacon, through the use of the lot. (For definitions, please see Glossary.)

The Formation Period

The early period of the Anabaptist movement (1525-1540s) was marked by ferment, reaction, and search for a common mind on the nature and patterns of church life. It is clear that the early Anabaptists assumed the need for spiritual leaders to serve as "shepherds" in the congregation. The Schleitheim agreement of 1527 lists the duties which fall to this office. It is not clear how early the threefold pattern of the ministerial offices was established. Harold Bender notes that it was well established by the time the *Strasbourg Discipline* was written in 1565 ("Ministry"—*Mennonite Encyclopedia*, Vol. III, p. 703).

Another window on their view of leadership appointments comes from the "Hans Holz" document in the "Berne Colloquy" of 1538:

Through our faith we have received grace and the apostolic office from God. However, we do not believe that all who believe and receive the faith in Christ should therefore be preachers. For these are different offices which are distinguished from each other but all belong to the same body.... We believe that there are a variety of gifts and offices. A person may not appoint himself; he must be chosen by the church" (Klaassen, *Anabaptism in Outline*, p. 125).

The elder or bishop was solely responsible for such functions as the administration of baptism, the Lord's Supper, and the ordination of other elders.

Women shared more actively in the life of the church in the Anabaptist congregations in the sixteenth century. Some exercised roles in evangelism, teaching, eldering, and writing ministries (*Leadership and Authority in the Life of the Church*, MPH, p. 9).

The Consolidation Period

For more than four hundred years (1540s-1945), the theology and patterns of ministry remained relatively constant. The threefold pattern of ministry (bishop-preacher-deacon) served as the common model for most congregations in North America. An implicit message was communicated that the ministry of the congregation was spiritually lodged in these offices. Persons were selected from the congregation by lot to serve for life.

The official *Ministers' Manual*, first published in 1890 by John F. Funk, defined the office of bishop in the following manner:

> The bishop or elder in the Mennonite Church is simply the minister who has been ordained to the special charge of caring for and officiating in the church of a prescribed district. This district may contain but one place of worship, or a number of places, which are at considerable distances from each other. He may have a number of fellow-ministers in his charge, to preach at the various places, and aid him in his work generally.

The authority of these leaders was rooted in the call of the congregation, authenticated by God through the use of the *lot*. Their role, by the twentieth century, was to oversee and to guide the life of the congregation. Their duties were defined through the use of biblical passages on ministry and from illustrations from early church life. Bishops were responsible for the spiritual and organizational life of the congregation, including church discipline. Preachers shared in the pulpit ministry, and deacons administered the alms fund. All shared in mutual counsel, visitation, and church discipline. The pattern of the district or "diocesan" bishop (H. S. Bender) emerged as these persons assumed responsibility for a number of congregations, some of which were "daughter" congregations emerging from their primary congregation.

The use of the lot among Mennonite Church congregations in North America was practiced into the middle of the twentieth century. Although the use of the lot was clearly established in the North American Mennonite colonies, there is no documentary evidence that it was used by the early Anabaptists in the selection of their spiritual leaders. The practice is rooted biblically in the selection of Matthias by the eleven apostles. The procedure was to nominate candidates who, as each nominee agreed, would be placed in the group. Books (usually Bibles) were placed in front of the candidates; one book had a slip of paper (the lot) in it. The slip said, "The lot has fallen into the lap of the one the Lord has chosen" (KJV). This phrase was drawn from Proverbs 16:33. Each nominee chose a book, and the one who received the book with the lot in it was ordained to the ministry.

The use of the lot reflected a high view of ministerial office and the view that one was called directly by God, not humans. The whole event had an aura of mystery and suspense. The outcome conferred a significant element of status and authority on the individual. The roots for this high view of office are similar to early Anabaptism which appears to be reflective of the attitudes of the Reformation faith groups from which our forebears came.

The second significant exploration of polity began in the 1925 session of the Mennonite General Conference of the Mennonite Church. At that time a committee was appointed to study the question of church polity. The committee recommended to the 1927 conference that "a committee be appointed to compile a work on church polity tending to help in the solution of difficult problems and unity of church regulation and government."

The committee that made the study was then appointed to compile a work on church polity. It's first draft was presented to the 1929 conference. This committee worked for a decade, sending out one revision after another for "examination and criticism." Finally, in 1941, a polity was presented and adopted by Mennonite General Conference (see Glossary). The book *Mennonite Church Polity* was published in 1944. Along with the polity, it included the Dordrecht Confession (1632), the Christian Fundamentals (adopted by Mennonite General Conference at Garden City, Mo., 1921), a set of gospel standards drawn up by the General Problems Committee of Mennonite General Conference (1939), the Constitution of Mennonite General Conference (1929, rev. 1943), and the *Minister's Manual* (published first in 1890 by John F. Funk).

Two sections from the 1941 Polity have relevance to this document: "IV. Church Members and Officers—Their Duties," and "V. Church Members and Officers—Their Responsibility and Discipline." Both articles begin with members and then move to bishops, ministers, and deacons. Article IV concentrates on how bishops, ministers, and deacons are ordained and then outlines their duties (Article IV also includes deaconess). Article V focuses largely on lines of accountability and, in turn, with ways to deal with failures and unfaithfulness.

This polity adopted and published in the midst of World War II seemed destined to a short life with minimal impact. The strong and unanticipated winds of change in both church and society following the war quickly made the polity obsolete, since it reflected the past and provided little guidance for the new day.

The Period of Change

Following World War II, major changes occurred in understandings about ministry within "Old" Mennonite groups at different times in conferences across North America. Most significant was the move away from "the bench" (bishop, minister, deacon) to a solo-pastor model. The 1950s and a decade or two following reflected major attitudinal shifts with a desire for organizational changes in congregational life. One of the significant shifts was the professionalization of ministry. *Call* was now related to an inner personal call plus seminary education in addition to the call from congregations. Therefore, ministers were often chosen from outside the congregation for terms of three to five years. With the change to a single-pastor system, partial or full financial support for pastors became more common.

In addition, large segments of the denomination appeared to be ready for change with respect to ministry offices and for the way ministry was organized. The traditional threefold pattern, with selection by the use of the lot, did not fit into contemporary expectations. The office of bishop began to disappear in part because of a growing reaction against the centralization of authority and power in this office. The role and function of deacon became ambiguous with the diminishing need to attend to the poor and to assist the bishop/minister with church discipline.

In the search for a new organizational model, the terminology of the office changed from *deacon* to *elder*, and these persons were normally selected for three-year time periods. In the process of change, the minister took on a more central role in the congregation with support from the elders group. In other cases, administration of the congregation fell increasingly to a church council comprised of members elected or placed in position through a gifts discernment process. In some cases, the church council began to view itself as a "board of directors" for the congregation with the pastor serving as their "employee."

These changes in the 1960s and 1970s coincided with societal changes which saw a gradual diminishing of respect for office; authority systems had less impact on group behavior, and ministry was defined, increasingly, in functionalist terms. The Recovery of the Anabaptist Vision movement contributed to such change by relocating the locus of ministry from the offices of ministry to the whole people of God. The phrase "priesthood of all believers" became the catch-phrase for this relocation of authority. The 1963 *Mennonite Confession of Faith*, Article 10, "The Ministers of the Church," also reflects the shift to a more functionalist view of ministry. It begins with a description of the "shepherds'" tasks and includes a concern for inclusion of all members in ministry, using "their spiritual gifts in its life and discipline." This Confession notes a more functionalist view of ordination to ministry (p. 18): "Ordination is ... symbolic of the church assigning responsibility and of God imparting strength for the assignment."

By 1971, the growing influence of district conferences and the reorganization of the Mennonite Church had a major impact on congregational life. Leadership responsibilities shifted from providing spiritual oversight and guidance to an emphasis on church program and administration; this shift was felt at all levels of denominational life.

The most dramatic shift occurred in the congregations with the introduction of the *church council*. Shifting responsibility for congregational life from the ordained leadership group to the lay leadership group brought a significant shift in congregational agenda. Church program and administration became the primary focus for congregational life.

The Reformulation Period

Adoption of the statement *Leadership and Authority in the Life of the Church* by the 1981 Mennonite Church General Assembly was a benchmark for the church in its attempt to reformulate its view of ministry and ordination. The document recognized the shifts that had occurred in the 1960s and 1970s and began cautiously to reformulate the church's position. It recognized the ministry of all persons, affirmed the importance of leadership ministries, and encouraged *shared* or *plural* ministry; it also recognized various terminologies for pastoral leaders.

The statement addressed such issues as leadership authority, congregational leadership patterns, conference-congregational relationships, and women in ministry. The statement on confirmation of leaders said that:

> ordination would then mean the act by which a person, after appropriate personal and corporate discernment, is formally and publicly appointed to a particular ministry in the life and/or mission of the church (pp. 39-40).

In 1984, an invitational Consultation on Leadership Polity (Stryker, Ohio) provided an opportunity to address further the questions of confirming and selecting leaders, congregational leadership models, and conference-congregation relationships. This meeting built on the assumptions contained in the "Leadership and Authority" document. The concept of ordination was affirmed. Plural ministry (leadership of the congregation shared by the ordained leadership and lay leaders) was assumed, but little clarity emerged about the place of the pastor in the congregation. However, the need for pastoral leadership was reaffirmed.

The most significant outcome of the 1984 consultation was a beginning corrective, or supplement, to the Mennonite Church's 1971 reorganizational statement regarding the relationship of the congregation to the conference and the denomination. It said:

There is general affirmation that a two-way flow of vision and agenda should characterize congregation, conference and denomination relations. The movement from the congregation to the ever-widening circles of conference and denomination reflects the centrality of the congregation in the life of the church. The conference and denominational agencies and bodies should be servants of each preceding circle of relationships. Simultaneously, the wider circles of conference and denomination can provide resources which challenge congregations to grow in faith and life.

The Ministry of All Members

The attempt to find a balance between the general ministry of all Christians and the particular ministry of ordained leaders is apparent in the more recent statements on the ministry which have emerged from the "Old" Mennonite Church in North America. There is a recognition that spiritual oversight and guidance, rooted in the Scriptures, should be maintained as a central role for those persons called to the offices of ministry. In part, this emphasis is recapturing the "Servant of the Word" perspective reflected in the writings of Paul M. Miller (*Servant of God's Servants*, 1964).

Recent Patterns of Pastoral Leadership

The 1982 and 1985 surveys of ministry by the Mennonite Board of Congregational Ministries (MBCM, Gordon Zook) identified three basic patterns and seven sub-patterns for congregational pastoral leadership in the Mennonite Church: pastoral leadership model, the "bench" model, and the team leadership model.

Recognizing that this research is dated, it may still bear some validity as a description for today. Surveys from 352 respondents in all regions of the church indicate that the "pastor leadership" pattern is representative of 66 percent of the church. "Bench" leadership (bishops, minister, deacon) is representative of 17 percent of the churches, mostly along the United States eastern seaboard. The "team leadership" model, including two to nine team members, is descriptive of about 11 percent of the congregations.

It is safe to assume that a pastoral leadership model (with one or more ordained leaders and three or more elders elected from within the congregation) is becoming the predominant pattern. This model, however, creates ambiguity about the authority and roles of the pastor and the church council. In part, it is a clash between an ecclesial (church) system and a secular democratic system. In addition, societal patterns of individualism have made members less willing to accept corporate authority, whether in the congregation or the broader church.

Women in Ministry

The early history of the Mennonite Church included women in congregational leadership roles. After several centuries of male leadership, the Mennonite Church in North America is again including women in congregational ministry roles. The Mennonite Church General Board appointed a Women in Leadership Ministries Committee in the mid-1980s to provide guidance to the church and to encourage area conferences to include women in pastoral leadership ministries through ordination. The 1986 Waterford "Statement of Convergence" said the following on the inclusion of women in ministry:

A majority of participants in the Waterford consultation favored equal eligibility of men and women for all ministries of the church. There was some dissent, however, from inclusion of women in ministries usually confirmed by ordination. The majority agreed on several words of exhortation to the church including:

(a) We acknowledge that we have not used fully the gifts of women in our church life.

(b) We encourage conferences who have not studied the issue of women in ministry to do so.

(c) We encourage conferences to approve the ordination of women for congregations requesting the same.

(d) We encourage our congregations and conferences to respect each other in their decisions regarding the ordination of women.

A 1989 report indicated that there are ordained, licensed, or commissioned women in ministry in all but five GC and MC district conferences. In addition, there are a significant number who are missionaries, administrators, and writers. A study in 1992 (MBCM, "Survey of Women in Pastoral Leadership," Sauder) of all women in both the General Conference Mennonite Church and Mennonite Church who held positions of ministerial leadership at some point from 1972-1992 indicates that the large-scale, successful entry of women into this traditionally male profession is giving women greater visibility and making a positive impact in both the Mennonite Church and the General Conference Mennonite Church. However, the survey also revealed that MC and GC congregations were calling women to pastoral ministry less frequently in the early 1990s than in the early 1980s.

It is noted here that there are also voices in both denominations which continue to exercise a biblical interpretation which reserves ordained ministry for men only. While this document unapologetically affirms the inclusion of women in all ministerial leadership offices, there is no intent to disrespect this "minority" viewpoint.

Ordination

In 1986, an invitational consultation (Waterford, Ind.) focused on *ordination* in the Mennonite Church. The "Convergence" statement, which resulted from the consultation, recognizes particular ministries normally associated with the pastoral office as calling for ordination, licensing, or commissioning. The conference and congregation share jointly in this confirmation process. The document defines who should be confirmed in these ways:

> Ordination is appropriate for continuing leadership ministries in the church, especially those which may include some ministry beyond the congregation or in behalf of congregations. Ministries of spiritual oversight typically confirmed by ordination or licensing may include apostles, prophets, evangelists, pastors, teachers, overseers-bishops, conference ministers, chaplains, deacons, conference or denominational administrators, etc.

Ministries of spiritual oversight typically confirmed by commissioning may include deacons, elders, youth leaders, congregational educators, conference or denominational administrators, etc.

Termination of ordination occurs by personal decision to resign the credentials; absence of task, gift, or sense of call; formal revocation by the conference or congregation for ethical unfaithfulness or incompatibility with Mennonite church doctrine and polity; by time or place limits agreed at the time of ordination.

Ministerial credentials may be transferred from one ministry setting to another as mutually agreed by the conferences, congregations, and/or agencies involved. Conference leadership committees and conference ministers are encouraged to continue their efforts to standardize procedures for transfer of credentials between conferences ("Convergence," 1986, p. 5).

Among the twenty-one area conferences which comprise the Mennonite Church of North America, practice varies around the confirmation of persons for ministry. Some conferences license persons for one or two years prior to ordination. Other conferences ordain persons to the ministry immediately upon being called to a congregational ministry assignment. The conference is involved in the ordination or licensing process, but it is normally not involved in the commissioning of persons as defined above.

Conference Role in Congregation-Pastor Leadership

Perhaps it is in the pastor placement process where the

conference-congregation polity is most visible. Congregations, accountable to other congregations in the conference, do not proceed alone in the calling and placement process:

> The conference should be represented by an area bishop, overseer, or conference minister in the discernment and confirmation of ordained ministries in congregational settings. During the call process, a conference leadership commission or personnel committee should assist in assessment of a candidate's readiness and qualification for the call under consideration. A conference minister or similar agent of conference is able to give invaluable counsel to committee, congregation, and candidate ("Convergence," 1986, p. 5).

The Pastorate Project

The Pastorate Project, sponsored by the Mennonite Board of Education, was a joint Mennonite Church/General Conference Mennonite Church effort to research both problems and possibilities for pastor-congregation dynamics and for developing congregational ministry leadership models.

The Pastorate Project manual for leaders who oversee pastors and congregations notes "four 'dimensions' of our church systems are particularly important" as they affect the pastorate (*Pastor-growing—People-growing*, p ix):

> 1. A pastor as an individual and in his or her relationships with the congregational leadership group, the congregation as a whole, and the larger church.

2. The congregational leadership group ("elders"/"deacons"/"lay ministers") in its relationships with pastor(s), congregation, and larger church.

3. The congregation as a whole in its relationships with pastor(s), leadership group, and larger church.

4. Support and accountability relationships of pastor(s), leadership group, and congregation with the larger church.

Although the Pastorate Project developed independently from the effort to frame this polity for ministerial leadership, several persons were involved in both projects. This provided good cross-fertilization and may have contributed to the convergence between the three leadership "dimensions" noted above (dimension #3 refers to the entire congregation and not just leadership) and the *threefold ministries* described in Section III. There are also some Pastorate Project proposals (such as the call to ordain elders to long-term service) which call for even more radical changes in congregational leadership structure.

On one central point, however, both projects concur: Mennonite congregations are most faithful to Anabaptist theology and traditions when leadership is provided by several people called out and confirmed by the congregation. The Pastorate Project coins the term "ministerial leadership team" (MLT) for such a group of leaders:

Crucial to the Anabaptist-Mennonite concept of the pastorate is the understanding that the responsibility for the leadership of the congregation is carried by a congregational leadership body, however this is called, and not by a single pastor alone (*Pastor-growing—People-growing*, p. xvii).

Ministry in Specialized Settings

The practice of the Mennonite Church varies considerably at this time. Some conferences grant ordination for persons in *specialized ministries* such as chaplains, pastoral counselors, Bible teachers, administrators of church institutions, etc. Some, however, take a functionalist view of ordination in limiting the confirmation to the duration of the person's service. Other conferences commission or license these persons who have not been ordained. In cases where persons were previously ordained, their ordination and ministry is confirmed by the conference for the particular ministry.

Vesting of Credentials

Unlike the General Conference Mennonite Church, which lodges ministerial credentials in its denominational office, credentials and recognition of ministerial status for Mennonite Church ministers are vested with each area conference. Even though ordination normally occurs in the context of the congregation, the congregation is not administratively responsible to maintain ordination records and credentials.

C. The General Conference Mennonite Church Story

Antecedents

The development of the General Conference Menno-

nite Church over the last 135 years is the complex result of church divisions, new immigrations, and moves
toward church unity. In order to fully understand the
history of this denomination as it relates to ministry
and ordination, it is necessary to go back to some of
the significant antecedents which helped to shape that
history.

The Northern European Mennonite Heritage

A dominant portion of what became the General Conference Mennonite Church is from immigrations growing out of the Dutch, North German, Prussian, and
Russian Mennonite community. While very much akin
to their Anabaptist kinsfolk of Switzerland, South Germany, and Austria, they contained within them some
unique influences which are significant antecedents to
what would emerge in ministry among the churches of
North America.

The first major shift in redefining ministry came
quite early among the more progressive Mennonites in
Holland. Education and urbanization seem to have
been key factors in the change which brought about a
call for a trained ministry and the call for the establish-
ment of a seminary already in 1675. The distinction between *elders* and *preachers* was first lost among the
Waterlanders when "in 1687 the elder died and the
three remaining ministers were authorized to perform
all functions on equal terms." With that, each pastor
became in effect a "full service minister" (Vollen-Di-
ener) no longer dependent upon an *Aeltester* (elder) for
baptism and communion.

It was a pattern which would be repeated in northern Germany, Prussia, later in the United States, and

still later in Canada among General Conference Mennonites. In each case, the pattern was for one trained minister to serve in each congregation, "ordained at once to serve as both preacher and elder and performing all functions in the congregations."

It is important here to note that this pattern is not some recent American innovation copying a Protestant model, as some have supposed. The pattern has strong roots in European Anabaptist antecedents of General Conference Mennonites. It should be noted, however, that the traditional pattern of elder/preacher/deacon continued in some churches alongside this innovation. The pattern came to prominence again in Russia and was brought from there to North America where it was influential in early General Conference practice and until recently in Canada.

The l847 Division in Pennsylvania

Among the issues related to the division within the Mennonite community in eastern Pennsylvania in l847 the issue of pastoral ministry cannot be ignored. John H. Oberholtzer was himself chosen by lot to the position of ministry at the relatively young age of thirty-four. With new responsibilities within the church, young Oberholtzer challenged some of the traditions around those who were in pastoral leadership, particularly by his initial refusal to wear the straight coat. But his concerns were more than to protest against traditions; his overriding concern was the reform and renewal of ministerial leadership, which he perceived at the time to be in a state of disrepute. Writing to the Mennonite community in Europe in l849, he said: "The one who gets the lot is then commissioned for ministry, be he ever so incompetent.... a large number of the ministers themselves have sunk to a low state of ignorance."

Instead of an open lot with many candidates, Oberholtzer suggested that the choice of ministers should be by one of three methods: (1) Election in the congregation; (2) by lot of the two most capable persons; or (3) directly by an inner impulse. Again writing to defend his reform movement, he said: "We have already obtained some of the most skillful speakers (thank God) whereas formerly, I think I can say four out of five were failures."

It has been argued (*Authority and Identity: The Dynamics of the General Conference Mennonite Church*, Sawatsky) that one way to understand the schism was around the changing understanding of ministry with a move toward what would result in the professionalization of ministry. Further evidence in this direction was the founding conference at West Point, Iowa, in May 1860 with Oberholtzer present, when the conference pledged "that an institution for theological training shall be established as soon as it can be accomplished."

General Conference Ministry Documents

Throughout the history of the General Conference Mennonite Church, there have been attempts to write out the policies and procedures for ministry; to briefly survey these documents is to gain an understanding of the ministerial polity and the practices of ordination as they have evolved over the 135 years of denominational history. In a 1957 presentation to a conference on ordination, S. F. Pannabecker called such documents "formularies." Until 1893, the basic sources were European in origin:

1. *Allgemeine Konferenz der Mennoniten von Nord-Amerika. Handbuch zum Gebrauch bei gottesdienstlichen Handlungen zunaechst fuer die Aeltesten und Prediger der Mennoniten-Gemeiden in Nord-Amerika* (Berne, Ind., 1893). Pannabecker identifies this as the first authorized document for ministry in the General Conference Mennonite Church. Three grades of ministry were recognized: deacons (Vorsteher), preachers (Prediger), and elder (Vollen Diener or Aeltester). Selection of these ministering persons was made by vote of the members of the congregation, with the lot as an option; ordination could follow that same day or later. Also recognized for ordination were the *Reiseprediger*, the *evangelist*, and the *missionary*.

2. *Forms of Service for the Use of Ministers* (Berne, Ind., 1908). This was a translation of the 1893 *Handbuch*, with some changes and adaptations. No longer was mention made of the lot. Deacons and ministers were ordained by handclasp while standing; elders were ordained while kneeling with the laying on of hands of all elders present.

3. *The Minister's Manual* (Newton, Kans., 1950). This was a major revision of the 1908 document, containing guidelines for ordination adopted by the General Conference Mennonite Church in 1945. It designates five varieties of service for which ordination is applicable: deacon, evangelist or licentiate, minister, elder, and missionary. The earlier clarity regarding the threefold ministry tradition is lost, though a second ordination is anticipated in the case of ordination as an elder. It presumes that women who are missionaries will be ordained, though not

as elders. This manual received a major revision in 1983, though now with the assumption of a single ordination for minister/elder.

4. *Procedures for the Ordination, Certification, and Registration of Ministers.* Practice often runs ahead of the guidelines, and such was the case as during the 1950s when pastors were increasingly being ordained in a single ordination as elder. These 1967 procedures were the attempt to catch up to the practice of the church and to offer to the General Conference Mennonite Church a more formalized set of expectations. For the first time, they introduced the concepts of licensing and commissioning in addition to ordination. They also made the assumption that the credentials for ministry would be vested at the denominational level, while the processing of the candidate would occur at the district/area conference level. In addition to procedures, there were also documents of *Standards of the Ministry and Definitions of Ordination, Commissioning, and Licensing.* While this set of procedures was widely accepted by the area conferences within the United States, they did not find acceptance or adoption within the provincial conferences of Canada.

5. *Understanding Ordination.* This is an official statement accepted by the General Conference Mennonite Church in 1974 at its triennial sessions. It legitimated a semi-functional understanding of ministry while still affirming the ministerial office concept. The primary significance of this document was the denominational endorsement of women being eligible for full ordination and the acceptance of persons having been divorced to continue in ministry.

Both of these items were very carefully and indirectly worded, but both effected substantial change within the General Conference Mennonite Church.

6. *Ordinal: Ministry and Ordination within the General Conference Mennonite Church, 1987.* For the fourth consecutive decade, issues of ordination again came to the forefront of ministry concerns. The primary significance of this document was its call for a return to the threefold ministry tradition by interpreting it in its contemporary form as the bishop tradition (conference ministers), the elder tradition (pastors and special ministries), and the deacon tradition (lay ministry). Area conferences in both the United States and Canada adopted the basic guidelines and put them into practice. The Ordinal also reflected a slight move away from the functionalist understanding of ministry to a more traditional acceptance of the office of ministry as important for accountability. It also provided for the first time a formal registration system of credentials within the denomination.

Education and Professionalization

Both within the antecedents and the actual history of the General Conference Mennonite Church, there has been a clear and strong move to call for specialized training for ministry; invariably, this has resulted in a significant degree of professionalization in the sense of one who has received training for ministry and is employed by the church most often on a full-time basis. Linked with that has been a clear call for accountability through credential-granting processes.

Women in Ministry

A unique form of ordination took place in the deaconess movement which had its origins among the Dutch and German Mennonites of Europe. Already in 1632, the Dordrecht Confession provided for the ordination of women who "are to visit, comfort, and take care of the poor, the weak, the afflicted and the needy ..., and further to assist in taking care of any matters in the church that properly come within their sphere, according to their best ability." Women who committed themselves to a life of Christian service worked in either congregations or other institutions of caring.

The 1945 General Conference Mennonite Church ordination guidelines provided for the ordination of missionaries who were women. Finally in 1974, the General Conference Mennonite Church passed a resolution committing the conference not to discriminate on the basis of sex (gender) when determining eligibility for ordination. Though steps were slow, there was certain support and movement in the last quarter of the twentieth century to ordain women to the office of ministry in the fullest sense of the word.

United States and Canada

As a church involved in more than one nation, it was perhaps inevitable that differing understandings and practices of ministry would emerge on the two sides of the border. The move toward an educated and professional ministry was a part of the General Conference Mennonite Church from its beginning. With the immigration of the Russian Mennonites to North America in the 1870s, there was a gradual acceptance of that model. In the United States, that transition was nearly completed by the end of World War II. On the Canadian side, with its substantial immigrations following both world wars, the movement toward education and professionalization was more gradual, with churches retaining the *Aeltester* and *minister* model in some cases into the present era. There is also on the Canadian side a strong tradition of *lay ministry*, working alongside of and with the trained professional pastor.

Vesting of Credentials

Though it has only been explicitly claimed in recent times, there has always been an assumed understanding in the General Conference Mennonite Church that ministerial credentials are vested in the denominational office. Throughout its history, the General Conference Mennonite Church has presumed within its authority the right to determine policies and procedures for ordination. Admittedly, the practice has been quite uneven with congregations at times claiming a tradition of congregational autonomy and thus carrying out ordinations within their own determination as to who and when. Generally, however, area conferences are responsible for processing ordinations and overseeing the work and ministry of those ordained, while the credentials themselves are vested in the denomination. Certificates of ordination are issued and permanent records are maintained at the denominational level. Furthermore, no transfer of credentials has been necessary once ordained within the General Conference Mennonite Church.

The Threefold Ministry Tradition

Though the story is mixed and sometimes confusing, it

is clear that the General Conference Mennonite Church has had a strong threefold ministry tradition. Daniel Hege was the first appointed *Reiseprediger* (traveling preacher), and as such served as one overseeing the congregations within his charge. With the redefinition of the elder (*Aeltester*) as an "overseer of congregations" to *elder* (*Aeltester*) as the "single full service minister of one congregation," it appears that the tradition of oversight ministry was lost. In Canada, this transition took place during the social turbulence of the 1960s. But experience demanded that the needs of the church be met with someone who had larger oversight responsibility than that of one congregation; thus the *conference minister* has emerged within the bishop tradition.

The minister as pastor of the local congregation has remained as an essential and the central focus of the ministry task.

In a similar manner, the *lay ministry* tradition has emerged in various forms but with a consistency which suggests that it is also bound up in the internal needs of the congregation. In Canada, it has continued explicitly under the rubric of "lay ministry." In some smaller congregations, they serve as pastors (sometimes in teams); elsewhere, they serve as pulpit assistants or as assistants to professional pastors. In the United States (and sometimes in Canada as well), the tradition is carried in some way by those who serve as *deacons* or, in some cases, as *elders*. Lay ministry is usually done gratis on a marginal time basis, and commonly by people without seminary training. Lay ministers may, or may not, be ordained; more commonly now, they are commissioned by the congregation. They are ministers in the congregation with responsibilities from the traditional roles filled by *deacons* (see Glossary).

Theology of Ministry and Ordination

With their greater cultural and social openness, North American Mennonites of northern European heritage (usually in the General Conference Mennonite Church) have often been receptive to the theological influences around them. In ministry, that has meant that the European and American sources of pietism helped shape understandings of the ministerial task. In the twentieth-century North American context, the theological debates centering around liberalism and fundamentalism often influenced pastoral leadership to choose among these competing ideologies. Later in the century, various strains of social activism with roots in both the right and the left of the political-social environment, often formed understandings of the minister's responsibility; these were normally perceived and interpreted as biblical ethical imperatives.

However, in the middle of the twentieth century, the influence of a functionalist theology of ministry became the dominant factor and was widely accepted by pastors within the General Conference Mennonite Church. Essentially, this understood ministry as matching the personal gifts of the identified leader with the perceived needs of the congregation. Ordination, if accepted at all, was understood as the temporary approval to exercise those gifts in the context of the congregation.

But viewed from the longer historical perspective, the more traditional theology of ministry and ordination has included a strong sense of the office of ministry. The ministerial office, which belongs to the church and not the individual minister, was granted by the church in the act of ordination and was intended to be a lifetime endowment as long as one faithfully served Christ and the church. Furthermore, ordination served as the link of accountability, for what had been given could also be taken away.

The Pastoral Call

The General Conference Mennonite Church has exercised considerable flexibility in its understanding of how one is called to ministry. Clearly, there has been a longstanding openness to that very personal call felt by the individual from God. But linked with that has been a strong sense that that personal call must be confirmed not once but continuously by the church.

Congregational Autonomy

The General Conference Mennonite Church history allows a modified form of congregational autonomy; decision-making responsibilities are accorded to the congregation as long as they do not harm the unity of the church. Providing such latitude for congregational decision making has been a way for the General Conference Mennonite Church to affirm congregational diversity as an asset, so as to enlarge and enrich the full body of Christ. However, where congregations have sought to grant or withdraw ministerial credentials without the involvement of the larger church on the basis of congregational autonomy, they have done so denying the spirit of congregational accountability which must always be held in a complementary relationship to notions of congregational autonomy.

D. Toward Convergence

History invites comparisons of the similarities and differences between General Conference and Mennonite Church polities relating to ministerial leadership. What unites and what still divides? What common experiences begin to point toward a common future for these two denominations? What belief systems serve as portents of unity in Christ's body, the church?

To focus the divisions of the past more pointedly: Can two Anabaptist traditions which have their separate rootages in southern and northern Europe now find their way to unity? Can two denominations which in part were formed out of a highly conflicted division around issues of ministry now find sufficient commonality to talk with each other about integration? Can two Mennonite groups who have formulated their responses to North American cultural influences around themes of separation and accommodation now find significant forms of both to lend unity and common commitments?

Or to ask the question in quite specific form: What are the signs that indicate some convergence in the two traditions around issues of ministerial polity?

1. **The threefold ministry tradition**. Clearly rooted in our common past has been some expectation that ministry will express itself in three forms. The story is uneven and the terminology used is often confusing, but in various ways we find ourselves returning to ministries of *oversight*, *pastoral leadership*, and some form of *lay ministry* (*elders or deacons*).

2. **The theology of ministry**. We are presently in the process of rethinking the theological foundations

upon which our understanding of ministry will rest. But even in the midst of these discussions, we also recognize some significant, recurring themes which both denominations affirm. These include: a strong belief that our ministry must be rooted in the ministry of Jesus Christ, that ministry must be centered in the life and mission of the church, that the gifts of the person must be linked to an office of ministry to sufficiently empower those who would serve in a representative role, and that accountability must be asked of those who receive the credentials of the church.

3. **Granting credentials**. Our heritage within the Anabaptist tradition makes us suspicious of those things which appear sacramental; for example, some ask whether "ordination" is appropriate language or an acceptable rite. However, there is a renewed consensus that we can authentically speak about licensing, ordaining, and commissioning servants of the church. Granting credentials is understood as the bonding of persons in ministerial leadership into a covenant of faith, bringing the person, the church, and God into continuing relationship.

4. **Linking congregations and conferences**. The General Conference Mennonite Church has traditionally emphasized the *congregation*, while the Mennonite Church has emphasized the *area conference*. (Neither denominational body is completely on one side or the other). Nevertheless, denominational gatherings for the General Conference Mennonite Church have been viewed primarily as a gathering of congregations (through congregational delegates), while churchwide gatherings for the Mennonite Church

have been a gathering of area conferences (through conference delegates).

Today *both* groups see the essential character of the church embodying both congregation and conference as forms of the church which must be linked in common ministry and mission. Both play an essential role in issues of ministerial polity when viewed from the long-term well-being of our church.

5. **Women in ministry**. While women were active in key leadership roles in the Anabaptist reformation, we have for generations been influenced by patriarchal systems which assumed that only men could be ordained and provide ministerial leadership. Today, both denominations are moving together to affirm that God calls, gifts, and empowers both women and men for leadership positions in the church.

6. **Professional ministry and lay ministry**. There exists within our two traditions two forms of ministerial leadership, both of which need to be claimed and reclaimed in the present time. Both forms existed side by side from the very beginning of the Anabaptist reformation, since several of the significant leaders of the reformation came from the ranks of the Catholic priesthood.

The *professional* ministry is that form which has received specialized training (normally in graduate seminary education), is salaried, is most often called to full-time employment by the church, and is granted credentials by the church. The *Ordinal* defines professional ministers as those who:
   • are trained to do the work,
   • are paid so they have time to do the work and

- are accountable to a group for the quality of the work done.

Another form, which often emerges in smaller congregations unable to support a full-time pastor, is *bi-vocational* ministry (see Glossary). While ordained to the ministry and perhaps even seminary-trained, the *bi-vocational* minister serves part-time and is employed in another vocation at the same time in order to earn an adequate income. The *lay* ministry (the ministry of unordained members) is that form which emerges out of the congregation through the affirmation of gifts, usually does not have seminary training, often requires another vocation, and thus is a position with a part-time commitment and often alongside a professional pastor. In some times and places and historical contexts, one or the other has emerged as dominant; when one form becomes dominant, it almost appears to be normative and necessary. In other times and places, the two have co-existed and served in a mutually supportive manner.

The Mennonite Church tradition and the General Conference Mennonites in Canada have been more rooted in the lay ministry tradition, but today, both have moved strongly to include the professional ministry as well. The General Conference Mennonite Church, particularly in the United States, has more often found itself moving toward the professional ministry, often to the exclusion of the lay ministry. Today, however, it is seeking to reaffirm the value and place for the lay ministry.

In certain times and places, forms of *anti-clericalism*

have emerged and helped to critique the professional ministry. When examples of unethical behavior occur in the life of ministers, when they assume authoritarian attitudes and assumptions about their status simply because of the office they hold, when arid intellectualism is substituted for authentic spirituality, or when expectations for personal gain exceed concern for those whom they serve, then the church has responded negatively to the professional ministry.

In other times and places, when the church has felt the necessity of calling for increased competence through education and adequate preparation, when the church has sensed a need for more full-time commitment to the demands of ministry, or when the church has sensed the need for greater clarity and differentiation and accountability on the part of its leadership, then the church has sought professional ministry as the anticipated answer. *Today, we cannot and should not value one more highly than the other; both professional ministry and lay ministry need to be seen as valid and valued forms of ministerial leadership. We most want to see them as two forms which complement each other and work together in harmony so as to contribute to the well-being and health of the church.*

E. Summary

These and other issues suggest that convergence is indeed already occurring with ministerial polity issues between the Mennonite Church and the General Conference Mennonite Church. There are, of course, also differences of both style and substance which remain. One response to the remaining differences will undoubtedly be tolerance and diversity. But the other answer is based upon the convergence which has already happened, sometimes to our own amazement. We remain confident that the Spirit of God who has begun a good work in us will bring it to completion in God's time if not in our time. To that end, we work toward a common polity for ministry so that our unity of faith and practice may bring to fulfillment the prayer of our Lord "that the world may believe."

A Mennonite Polity for Ministerial Leadership

A. Introduction

The purpose of polity is to enhance the exercise of ministry so that the church is blessed and God is glorified. While all members are ministers, this polity describes several ministerial offices which are vested with the authority to lead a congregation.

A Mennonite polity understands the relationship between congregations and their ministerial leaders and the relationship between congregations within the conferences/denomination to be one characterized by covenant with each other before God. The relationship, built on promises made, is one of interdependence and mutuality. This covenant is affirmed each time a congregation joins the conference/denomination. It is made real in the ongoing life of the church as it lives out its common confession of faith and as it carries out programs that were decided upon jointly.

As Mennonites, we desire to live with each other in a covenant relationship. "You are the body of Christ, and individually members of it" (1 Cor. 12:27, RSV). We want connections which help us be accountable to each other for our life and mission. The governance aspect of polity flows out of this understanding of and respect for covenant. Covenants, which are made voluntarily, lie at the heart of Anabaptist understandings of the church.

Governance authority granted to leaders, then, is in the context of this larger covenant between the constituent elements of church: congregation, conference, and denomination. Authority is built on a strong sense of mutual accountability (Heb. 13:17). Those chosen to lead are given support, but they also are accountable. They are entrusted with authority with the understanding that they too are under authority. Leaders are accountable within the congregation, but also beyond it within the whole church. Both ordination and installation are covenanting services between the minister and the congregation, made in the presence of God. All members make a covenant at the time of baptism.

The ministerial leadership polity that grows out of this covenant relationship recognizes three offices of ministry:

1. Oversight ministries (conference ministers, overseers, and a denominational department of ministerial leadership).

2. Pastoral ministries.

3. Deacon/elder ministries.

Congregational leadership, then, is a responsibility shared by persons duly discerned and called to these three offices; it is worked out within a spirit of mutuality and covenant. Normally, pastors and those called to offices of oversight are ordained, while those called to the role of deacon/elder are usually not ordained.

In setting this polity alongside the three main polities of other communions, we find that it shares some characteristics with each of them, but is also distinct from each.

Episcopal: This polity has a more hierarchical structure, with the preponderance of authority resting with the bishops, especially historically. The emphasis on apostolic succession (see Glossary) reinforced this clergy-centered authority. In modern times, the laity have been increasingly included in the councils where decisions are made.

Presbyterian: This tradition accords leadership authority to a group of elders (presbytery) which is comprised of lay and clergy members representing a group of congregations. Decisions made at this level are subject to revision by the two higher bodies, namely the synod and the general assembly. Ministerial credentials are processed at the presbytery level.

Congregational: Churches which are ordered through a congregational polity (e.g., Southern Baptist) invest decision-making authority primarily in the congregation. Conferences or assemblies of congregations within this polity generally have only advisory power over any one congregation.

A **Mennonite polity** respects and takes seriously the congregation, but understands church to include conferences and the denomination in North America. Authority is shared and exercised at the various levels. Such a polity is intended to serve not only in ordering the ministerial leadership of the congregation but also the polity for ministerial leadership in area conferences and in an integrated Mennonite denomination in North America, as well. Over the past decades, there has been increasing conversation and cooperation between the General Conference Mennonite Church and the Mennonite Church. Ministers from both traditions have "crossed over," and now serve faithfully. This increasing interaction and growing convergence of procedures/structures calls for a common polity for ministerial leadership (see Section II, and also *Confession of Faith in a Mennonite Perspective*).

Attempting to describe a polity for General Conference and Mennonite Church congregations in North America requires a careful understanding of each tradition and the leadership polities which evolved (see Section II) separately. We now describe a ministerial leadership polity for both groups in the future, as the two denominations continue to work together cooperatively and will eventually merge.

B. The Threefold Ministries

Oversight Ministries (Denominational and Conference)

At the denominational level, there will be a *department of ministerial leadership* to provide overall direction, coordination, and support to the pastoral leadership system and to ministerial persons serving the church. Cooperating offices of this department may function in different geographical locations to serve regional areas, existing denominational bodies, or countrywide structures and needs.

These offices are responsible to provide resources (guidelines for ministry, ministerial transition materials, information services) and assistance (consultation and in-service training) to those persons in area conferences (usually called conference ministers) who provide oversight and care for the pastor-congregation system.

The *department of ministerial leadership* will supply procedures for granting ministerial credentials. It plans settings for discussions with and training for conference ministers to unify practice in granting and maintaining credentials, and for professional growth and development. These offices keep files/profiles of those who carry ministerial credentials and lists each minister's status and current place of service. It is accountable to the churchwide gathering of conferences through whatever board, commission, or committee has been duly established by the denomination.

Each conference appoints a *conference minister*. The conference minister relates to and carries out the policies and concerns of the ministerial committee (or comparable group) of the conference. This generally means giving oversight to congregations and pastors. This oversight consists of assisting in granting/withdrawing of credentials, pastoral transitions, and establishing guidelines for ministry. It also means working with district *overseers*, where there are such, by being a resource in their work. The conference minister(s) is accountable to the conference through the structure established by that particular area conference; these accountability structures may vary significantly. The overall concern is for the spiritual vitality and well-being of both pastors and congregations.

In some area conferences, *overseers* or *bishops* may be appointed to serve a geographical cluster of congregations. They are chosen and affirmed by conference ministerial leadership persons along with the pastors and congregations they serve. Overseers or bishops are present to give ongoing counsel to congregations and pastors, including times of congregational and leadership review, transitions, terminations, or when special outside resources may be needed. The overseer or bishop utilizes the resources of the conference minister. (Note: The term "overseer" is problematic for some Mennonites, especially African-Americans with ancestors who were enslaved by "overseers.")

Boundaries and Connections: Personnel at the denominational offices and conference offices respect each other's roles and work together for the well-being of the organizations, congregations, and those in ministerial positions.

Pastoral Leadership

Pastors who have been granted a credential by the area conference serve in the congregation to which they are called. Their tasks may include preaching, teaching, pastoral care and counseling, giving leadership to the administration of the ordinances, equipping all members to ministry, and other activities which foster health and growth of the congregation.

Boundaries and Connections: Pastors respect each member of the congregation where they serve and are accountable to the congregation for agreed-upon tasks. They are approved by the conference for service in that congregation and receive oversight from the conference, are supportive of each other, and where possible meet with others from their geographical area on a regular basis for prayer, mutual care, and encouragement.

Elders/Deacons/Lay Ministers

Elders are chosen in some congregations to do pastoral care with the pastor, creating a ministerial leadership team, providing spiritual oversight of the congregation, and serving as a support group for the pastor. *Deacons* serve in some congregations (sometimes ordained) to assist the pastor and are often given responsibility for looking after those in financial need. *Lay ministers* (General Conference) are persons chosen for their gifts in ministry, may or may not have theological training, and may or may not be salaried. They often serve smaller congregations or assist the lead pastor in larger congregations.

Elders/deacons/lay ministers are chosen from the congregation because they demonstrate gifts for ministry and exemplary moral character. They may do pastoral care, preach, look after the needy, and provide encouragement and support for the pastor(s).

Boundaries and Connections: Elders, deacons, and lay ministers serve within the congregation according to the understandings established by the area conference of which the congregation is a part. They complement the pastor's ministry (where there is a pastor) and are accountable to the congregation through periodic reviews. The goal is that every congregation experience committed, caring, spiritual leadership.

C. Forms of Recognition

Women and men may be granted *credentials* to Christian ministry. These credentials are granted only by the area conference, but are respected by all Mennonite congregations, and conference and churchwide organizations. The credential is granted by a conference, and the credentialed person is accountable to the conference for the ministry credential.

Licensing Toward Ordination. This licensing credential is given for a two-year period of time and can be renewed for a second two-year term. The licensing period is not only a time of testing God's call to ministry but also is a period when the church can support the candidate so that he/she will succeed in the ministry.

Ordination for Ministry. A long-term continuing ministry credential granted by the church to serve in a representative capacity within the church's ministerial office. Ordination usually follows the period of time designated by the ministerial *license*. The conference provides guidance for the congregations in the discernment and ordination process. The appropriate leadership group in the congregation and the overseer or conference minister will consult with the candidate and together plan a process to discern the readiness for ordination. While the conference is responsible for the ordination credential, the conference leadership group needs counsel from the congregation and candidate in order to make a good decision. Consideration is given to performance, relationship skills, aptitude, theology, and commitment. This information is gathered by interviews and/or written materials. An ordination ceremony is planned by the congregation in consultation with the conference and the person to be ordained. Conference personnel (often conference minister or overseer) are involved in the ceremony to symbolize the covenant relationship between minister, congregation, and the wider church.

Licensing/Commissioning for Specific Ministry. This credential is time-specific, location-specific, and/or ministry-role specific. It is not intended to move toward ordination. The credential continues as long as the person is engaged in the ministry task, such as youth ministry, a role in a church institution, or a lay ministry role. While this credential is given to a person who may be serving in an institution other than the congregation, the request for licensing/commissioning should be processed with the congregation and the conference.

Why do we suggest alternative terms for this third ministry credential? In some parts of the church, the term "licensing" is preferred; in other parts of the church, the term "commissioning" is preferred. In either case, this preference is identified by which term is deemed to carry greater meaning, authority, and clarity. Area conferences will need to determine which of these will prevail in their common usage.

There is another form of commissioning which is not officially a ministry credential but is the *blessing* of the church for a special task or role. This commissioning is congregation-based and does not require conference action. Congregations may choose to commission persons such as elders/deacons, missionaries, voluntary service workers, or persons who are called to specialized tasks.

Accountability

Persons who are granted credentials are accountable in various ways to the church. The following diagram illustrates the accountability flow for pastors, chaplains, and those in oversight ministries (overseers, bishops, conference and denominational offices):

	For Christian Life & Faith	Job Performance	Credentials	Professional Standing
Pastor	Congregation (& conference)	Congregation	Conference (& congregation)	Professional Organization
Chaplain	Congregation (& conference)	Employing Agency	Conference (& congregation)	Professional Organization
Oversight Minister	Congregation (& conference)	Conference/ Denomination	Conference (& congregation)	Professional Organization

Accountability is the dynamic whereby a minister submits and subjects his/her ministry, faith, and life to the church. The offices of ministry are great treasures of the church; each person placed in a ministerial office is a steward of this treasure, humbly and openly providing an account of the ways he/she manages this trust.

A distinction is drawn, however, between accountability for *job performance* and *Christian life and faith*. For example, a chaplain is responsible to his/her employer for *job performance*. But because the chaplain represents the church in this extra-congregational role, the congregation and conference establish support and review systems which monitor the chaplain's *Christian life and faith*. Such accountability is also expected of others who hold ministerial credentials for roles outside the congregation (i.e., missionaries, conference staff, and those ordained to denominational offices).

Who Grants Ministerial Credentials and for What?

Ministerial credentials are granted, according to established guidelines, by the area conference where the person serves, resides, or holds congregational membership. Ministerial credentials indicate that a person is gifted and qualified for a particular ministry to which she or he has been called. All pastors are ordained or licensed; deacons and lay ministers may be commissioned.

Conferences may also grant ministerial credentials to those serving in ministry beyond the congregation: chaplains, Bible teachers, seminary professors, mission workers, and persons with assignments in church organizations and institutions. Those in denominational offices, conference offices, or who are overseers may also be ordained. These persons follow the same procedures as pastors in receiving credentials. Request for credentials for specialized ministry comes jointly from the candidate's congregation and the organization served (or to which the person is accountable). Persons with credentials for specialized ministries are accountable for the credential to the conference which granted the credential, or to the conference in which they reside.

How a Person Receives Ministerial Credentials

Ministerial leadership credentials are granted to those persons who sense a call to Christian ministry; are affirmed by their congregation for their gifts, character, and commitment; and are approved by the area conference ministerial leadership committee. A credential is granted only to those who have a place of service.

1. *License for Ministry—Leading Toward Ordination.* A ministerial license grants the person all the privileges and responsibilities accorded to an ordained person, except to ordain someone else. The license is issued for a two-year period for the purpose of further discerning ministerial gifts, abilities, and aptitude. It may be extended for another two-year period if more discernment time is needed. A license for ministry is not transferable to another area conference or denomination.

To request the license for ministry, the following items should be submitted to the area conference ministerial committee:

a. a letter of request from the candidate's congregation for the person to be licensed,

b. a copy of the *Ministerial Leadership Information* form which had been completed for the search process, and

c. a theological statement or response as requested by the area conference committee.

These materials are studied by the appropriate conference committee prior to a personal interview with the candidate. This committee will follow with their response, either approving or denying the request for licensing. They may also designate additional reading, academic courses, or other requirements to be completed during the licensing period prior to consideration for ordination. In addition, the area conference ministerial committee will designate an experienced pastor within the Mennonite church to serve as a pastoral mentor to the licensed person for the duration of the licensing period.

Within the context of a worship service in the congregation, an appropriate ceremony recognizing the granting of the licensing credential should be observed. A person representing the area conference ministerial committee should be present and participate in this recognition. Because of the preliminary nature of this credential, this ceremony is normally minimal, anticipating the greater observance in ordination.

2. *Ordination.* Ordination is the appropriate credential

for pastors, overseers, conference ministers, bishops, chaplains, missionaries, evangelists, those serving in the denominational department of ministerial leadership, and those determined by the church to have a continuing, representational, ministerial leadership role in and on behalf of the church. Ordination to the church's office of ministry grants to the person the full range of ministerial privileges and responsibilities.

Ordination normally follows in the period during which the candidate holds a license, with initiation of the process during the second year. Preparation for ordination will include assessment and reflection on the person's ministry within the congregation, with the conference minister or overseer, and with the pastoral mentor.

To request ordination for ministry, the following items should be submitted to the area conference ministerial committee:

a. a letter of request from the candidate's congregation for the person to be ordained, including a brief report of their discernment process,

b. a statement of the candidate concerning the meaning of ordination, its privileges and responsibilities, and the accountability relationships contingent upon it,

c. a written report and statement of support from the pastoral mentor, and

d. an updated theological statement or response as requested by the area conference committee.

These materials are studied by the appropriate conference committee prior to a personal interview with the candidate. It is recommended that a representative from the congregation participate with the candidate in the interview with the area conference committee. This committee will follow with their response, either affirming or denying the request for ordination.

Within the context of a worship service in the congregation, the ceremony of ordination should be celebrated as a special and significant occasion for both the congregation and the person being ordained. A person representing the area conference ministerial committee—usually the conference minister, overseer, or bishop—should be present and participate in this ceremony. Other pastors and persons representing the larger church community should be invited as well (see "Forms of Recognition" on page 79).

3. *License/Commission for Specific Ministry.* A ministerial license grants the person all the privileges and responsibilities accorded to an ordained person, except to ordain someone else. This ministerial credential is issued for the duration of a particular term of service. It may be limited in time, position or role, or by geographical location; and it is not transferable to another area conference or denomination.

To request the license/commission for ministry, the following items should be submitted to the area conference ministerial committee:

a. a letter of request from the candidate's congregation for the person to be licensed/commissioned,

b. a statement of the candidate concerning the meaning and purpose of this license/commission, and

c. a theological statement or response as requested by the area conference committee.

These materials are studied by the appropriate conference committee prior to a personal interview with the candidate. This committee will follow with a response, either approving or denying the request for licensing/commissioning.

Within the context of a worship service in the congregation, an appropriate ceremony recognizing the granting of the licensing/commissioning credential should be observed. A person representing the area conference ministerial committee should be present and participate in this recognition.

Credentials for Youth Ministry

A person who senses God's call to youth ministry, is confirmed by the congregation and the appropriate conference authorities, and anticipates a long-term ministry with youth may follow the licensing and ordination procedure. This call and provision for a credential is carefully discerned in each situation and is considered the normal procedure when the person is employed as a youth minister.

Persons who intend to serve in youth ministry for a short time receive some recognition for this role other than through formal licensing and ordination. Consideration should be given to "License/Commission for Specific Ministry" or to a simple commissioning of the congregation.

Maintaining Ministerial Credentials

The area conference holds the credentials of all licensed, ordained, and licensed/commissioned persons serving in that conference. A form is completed for each person with information on dates of the license, ordination, place of service, and current status. It is the responsibility of the area conference to provide supervision and accountability for all persons holding credentials in their conference.

The denominational department of ministerial leadership maintains a record of all persons with ministerial credentials. This is a collection from all the conferences. Conferences annually inform the denominational office of all ministerial credential changes. Deaths of those with ministerial credentials will be reported to this office. The denominational office will publish the list (in the annual Handbook/Yearbook) of all persons who have been granted credentials by area conferences.

Credentials by Ministerial Role

I. Oversight Ministries

    A. Licensed Toward Ordination—not normally used for Oversight Ministry

    B. Ordination

        1. Ordained and serving in a denominational ministerial leadership office. IB1

        2. Ordained and serving as a conference minister. IB2

        3. Ordained and serving as an overseer, bishop. IB3

    C. Licensed/Commissioned for Specific Ministry. IC

II. Church and Pastoral Ministries

A. Licensed Toward Ordination—initial ministry role within denomination. IIA

B. Ordination

1. Ordained and serving as a lead pastor in a congregation—co-pastors. IIB1

2. Ordained and serving as an associate/assistant pastor in a congregation—youth minister. IIB2

3. Ordained persons serving in a ministry in specialized settings:

   a. Chaplain/pastoral counselor. IIB3a

   b. Missions and/or service assignment. IIB3b

   c. Conference or church administrator—conference youth minister. IIB3c

   d. Teacher in a church educational institution. IIB3d

C. Licensed/Commissioned for Specific Ministry. IIC

1. Licensed/Commissioned and serving as a lead pastor in a congregation—co-pastors. IIC1

2. Licensed/Commissioned and serving as an associate/assistant pastor in a congregation—youth minister. IIC2

3. Licensed/Commissioned persons serving in a ministry in specialized settings:

   a. Chaplain/pastoral counselor. IIC3a

   b. Missions and/or service assignment. IIC3b

> c. Conference or church administrator—conference youth minister. IIC3c
>
> d. Teacher in a church educational institution. IIC3d

III. Lay Ministries (i.e., Elders, Deacons, Lay Ministers)
Some, though not all, may carry a ministry credential—use subcategories identified under II. More often they will be commissioned in a noncredentialed manner within the congregation.

Categories of Credentials

License Toward Ordination (LTO). A two-year license granted for the purpose of discerning ministerial gifts, abilities, and aptitude.

Ordination for Ministry

Active (OAC). The continuing ministry credential held by those holding a charge for ministry.

Active Without Charge (OAW). The credential held by those not presently holding a charge for ministry (for a period of up to three consecutive years after which the credential status becomes Inactive).

Inactive (OIN). The credential held by those who have been without a charge for more than three consecutive years or who have left the denomination. This credential is not valid for performing ministerial functions. The conference which holds this credential is not responsible for the actions of a person so recognized. If, subsequently, an invitation to a ministerial assignment is received, the area conference ministerial committee will be informed and an interview will be conducted to decide whether to reactivate the ordination credential.

Retired (ORE). The credential held by those who have retired from active ministry. This credential is valid for performing ministerial functions and is to be exercised with discretion. A retired credential is available to persons at least fifty-five years of age.

Probation (OPR). The credential held by those having a charge for ministry who are placed under close supervision for a specified period of time in order to determine whether the credential will be continued. At the conclusion of the probationary period, it is determined whether the credential becomes Active, Suspended, or Withdrawn.

Suspended (OSU). The credential for ministry is laid aside for a specified period of time for disciplinary reasons. At the end of the suspension period, it is determined whether the credential becomes Active or Withdrawn. Suspended credentials are not valid for performing ministerial functions.

Withdrawn (OWI). This is the designation used when disciplinary action is taken to remove the ministerial credential and that which was given in ordination.

Terminated (OTE). This is the designation used when a ministry credential is ended for nondisciplinary reasons upon approval of the area conference ministerial leadership committee.

Transferred (OTR). This is the designation when an Active or Active Without Charge credential is transferred to another denomination.

Deceased (ODE).

Licensed/Commissioned for Specific Ministry (L/CSM). A credential granted for the duration of a particular term of service, which may be limited in time, position, role, or geographical location.

The Transfer of Credentials

When an ordained person moves to another area conference, the new conference requests the transfer of the credential. It is incumbent upon the conference in which the minister has served to review the minister's experience and determine whether the minister's credential is in good standing for transfer. The conference where he or she served will furnish a copy of the minister's registration information form (or ministry service record) and a letter of recommendation (after reviewing the minister's standing) to the requesting conference. The denominational office will receive a copy of this correspondence. Upon transfer of the ministerial credential, the new conference shall be solely responsible for maintaining the credential through its supervision and accountability structure.

Ministers from Other Denominations

Ministers ordained in other Christian denominations are required to complete the same process as anyone who seeks credentialing for Mennonite ministry.

Assuming approval for ministry, a two-year license is granted and may be renewed for an additional two years. A pastoral mentor will be assigned. Such a licensing period allows for a time of mutual discernment as to whether this is a ministry relationship which will benefit both the church and the ministering person. It also allows time for an appropriate check and transfer of ordination credentials by the conference/denomination.

The licensed person will be expected to affirm and teach Anabaptist-Mennonite faith after doing prescribed study and reading in Mennonite history, theology, and ecclesiology. He/she is required to attend conference sessions as well as pastoral peer groups.

Following the satisfactory completion of the licensing period, a covenant ceremony which affirms the person's previous ordination will take place. At that time a Mennonite certificate of ordination will be granted by the conference.

D. The Calling and Locating of Pastors

Persons in pastoral ministry are part of the congregation where they serve and thus a part of the broader church and its life. They receive their call through the church and are accountable to the broader church through the area conference in which they reside.

The Call to Ministry

Potential pastors have a sense of call to serve Christ and the church effectively. A vital, living faith in Christ and a deep desire for the well-being of the church are essential. A person sensing a call from God to ministry also receives the discernment of the church regarding his or her gifts for ministry. Those who live and work with the person can bring the most helpful observations. Congregations are active in identifying and encouraging men and women to consider pastoral ministry. This is often done by "shoulder-tapping" young persons (and even older members who have shown they have the required gifts) and inquiring whether they sense God's call in their lives to minister. The congregation also helps with the decision process and places the candidate in touch with the overseer or conference minister.

Persons who sense a call to ministry prepare themselves through formal studies including biblical, theological, pastoral care, mission, and the work of the church. (See "Preparation for the Respective Ministries," p. 96) Those in oversight positions encourage these persons to attend Mennonite institutions of learning.

Finding the Right Place

Each area conference establishes procedures for helping those in pastoral ministry find a location for ministry. Congregations, like pastors, have personalities. Therefore, careful consideration is given in the calling of a pastor. In the discernment process, attention is given to the pastoral gifts and the needs in the congregation. Much prayer and intentional work is required. (See "Ministry Transition Packet" from the denominational department of ministerial leadership.)

Conference personnel are very important to this process. The conference minister or overseer is fully involved in these times of transition. They encourage the congregation to consider both women and men for pastoral positions.

E. Relationships Which Provide Resources for Ministry

All persons in ministry need a structure to provide resources and accountability. Those persons in oversight ministries (conference ministers, overseers) faithfully carry out the tasks assigned them. They report to those in the structure to whom they are accountable and welcome feedback from those they serve.

Persons serving in the denomination's department of ministerial leadership fulfill the responsibilities given them. Periodic and ongoing review of work is conducted according to assigned ministerial tasks. Fair employment guidelines are followed.

The conference minister and overseer fulfills his or her responsibilities assigned by the conference. Periodic and ongoing review will be conducted according to the assigned oversight tasks. Fair employment guidelines are followed.

Persons in pastoral ministry respect the denomination and conference authority. They serve faithfully in the place where they are called and according to the ministerial assignment. Periodic reviews of their work are conducted with the counsel of the overseer/conference minister. Fair employment guidelines are followed. These guidelines are often provided by area conferences.

Elders (deacons and lay ministers) share the task of leading the congregation with the minister and are accountable to the congregation through its structures. Description of assignments are provided by the congregation, and evaluations are to be done in accordance with the assignment.

A person ordained to a specialized ministry also needs resources and accountability. This will happen through the conference office, either by a direct relationship or through the congregation where he or she is a member. A clear understanding of this relationship will be established at the time of giving the credential or when the person moves into the assignment.

Preparation for the Respective Ministries

Preparation is essential for persons involved in pastoral and specialized ministry. The type and extent of preparation are considered in light of the assignment. Those preparing for ministry should study at Mennonite educational institutions to provide adequate understanding of Mennonite theology and practice. A Master of Divinity is the standard degree, but the extent of the training will be determined by the group which does the examination for ministry and the congregation to be served. A person may be denied a credential or be required to complete a certain course of study before a credential is granted. The period of licensing allows for time to do further preparation before the ordination credential is granted.

It is also essential that all persons in ministerial assignments participate in continuing education appropriate to their ministry to enhance their ability to serve. The congregation or institution they serve should encourage and provide financial support for this endeavor. Continuing education may consist of study leaves, directed studies, peer-group counseling, part-time study at a nearby institution, and attendance at seminars and conferences planned by the Mennonite church and its conferences. Conference ministers and overseers will help persons in pastoral ministry plan for these studies.

Ministerial Review

Ministerial leadership reviews and other forms of informal response to those in leadership positions are inevitable, natural, and always present. The goal is to conduct formal reviews in a responsible manner that contributes to the health and well-being of both the congregation and the pastor.

The basic purpose of a ministerial review is to facilitate growth toward more effective ministry. Such growth is more related to affirmation and support than to critique and negative evaluations; it is also more oriented to the future than to the past. While identifying weaknesses and problem areas and taking them seriously, the assumption should be that the minister will also build upon existing strengths rather than focusing entirely upon correcting weaknesses.

It may be unwise to undertake a review process when other major issues are being addressed by the congregation and/or conference. Also, if significant conflicts are present, they should be addressed separately and prior to any formal review. Reviews almost never resolve conflicts but rather tend to escalate them.

At some points it is appropriate to review the congregation or conference system as part of, or alongside, the review of persons with ministerial leadership responsibility. To cast these toward a more positive direction with an eye to the future, it may be helpful to do such reviews in the context of goal setting.

It is recommended and strongly encouraged that consultation services be sought from either conference sources or other qualified consultants when carrying out ministerial reviews. Healthy reviews and subsequent decisions regarding continuing relationships are often dependent upon the involvement, wisdom, and full participation by the pastor, the congregation, and the conference.

F. Search for Wholeness in Ministry

The polity described here is intended to give direction toward wholeness in ministry. Ministers with spiritual, emotional, physical, and social health contribute to a healthy growing church. Each person, regardless of his or her place in the church, should assume the responsibility to work at wholeness for self and others. This is Shalom.

Section IV.
Qualifications for Ministry

Introduction

Qualifications for ministry fall into three major categories: personal character, membership, and suitability for the task and/or function. The purpose of ministry is to bear fruit in the service of God. It is assumed, therefore, that a person cannot have a vital, living ministry without a personal growing faith in Christ.

Because it is the church which establishes and nurtures settings for ministry, the church is, therefore, finally responsible for the settings in which ministries lead the church. The church recognizes and values such ministry settings and describes them as *ministerial offices* (see Section I). It is usually expected that any person called to serve in such an office will hold membership for at least one year in a Mennonite congregation and give clear evidence of a deep commitment to that community of believers.

No one person will have command of all gifts and/or skills made available by Christ for ministry in the church. Thus, the qualifications for ministry also presume that specific skills and talents will be recognized and identified in individuals for the purpose of matching them to those ministries which are best suited to their own particular gifts and talents.

Personal Character: Relationship to God, to Self, and to Others

Qualifications for ministry begin with one's new birth

into a living and abiding *relationship with God* through Christ. Ministry presumes that a person is committed to Christ and the church through believer's baptism, has a membership covenant with a Mennonite congregation, and subscribes to the current Mennonite Confession of Faith. A genuine disciple of Christ is one who covenants to walk with Christ, expressing a dynamic and growing faith through consistent and regular devotion to the Word, prayer, fellowship with other believers, practicing obedience to Christ's commands, and being willing to give and receive counsel in the body of Christ.

The New Testament's pastoral epistles outline qualifications for the ministry. One must be above reproach, faithful to one spouse, temperate, sensible, respectable, hospitable, an apt teacher, not a drunkard, not violent but gentle, not quarrelsome, and not a lover of money. A minister must care well for his/her own household, because that is the foundation of being able to care pastorally for the church. A minister must not be a recent convert and must be well thought of by those outside the church. He/she must treat older women respectfully like a mother, younger women like sisters, younger men like brothers, and older men like fathers. These pastoral relationships are to be characterized by courtesy, honor, respect, and purity (1 Timothy).

A minister must understand that there will be times of stress. The aim must be righteousness, faith, love, and peace. Stupid and senseless controversies are to be avoided, and opponents should be corrected with gentleness. A minister must be grounded in the Scriptures, using them for teaching, reproof, correction, and training. This calls for persistent proclamation of the message and the ability to convince, rebuke, and encourage with utmost patience in teaching (2 Timothy).

A person with a healthy self-image demonstrates a realistic self-understanding coupled with emotional stability and a clear sense of self-worth; this self-worth finds its source in Christ. The ability to cope with stress and conflict is evident in the minister's personal life. Likewise, flexibility, adaptability, and general maturity are reflected in the person's response to life's difficulties and trials. A minister's life also provides evidence of personal character being transformed into Christ-likeness. Evidences of such personal transformation include the fruit of the Spirit (as described in Gal. 5:22-26) and the blessings of the Christian character described in the Beatitudes of Matthew 5. A general attitude of humility, openness, and integrity—nurtured by one's faith in Christ, hope in his return, and love for God and the church—describes the person's developing character.

A kind and friendly nature is generally expected of those called to the ministry. Key and intimate friendships are developed with others; such relationships are signs of maturity, vulnerability, and relational stability. A general attitude of acceptance, forbearance, and forgiveness toward others is consistently displayed in interpersonal relationships.

Qualifications Relating to Office and/or Role: Personal Validation and Validation by the Church

An authentic *personal call* is presumed; the person has a clear inner calling to the ministry. The individual will have walked a path of discernment, tested his or her own heart and mind in this regard, and will have received personal verification. Questions as to how or why one believes one has been called to the ministry have been answered. (For example: "Do I have a spirit of servanthood, or am I simply out for a position of power?" or, "Do I have a proper sense of the nature of the work, or am I simply looking for prestige and recognition?")

Likewise, the candidate for ministry will begin to have a clearer sense of the responsibilities involved; these include the self-discipline and motivation required to remain faithful to the task of the call as well as to the *call* itself. As a result, the full implications of the requirements, expectations, and demands of the call will be clearly understood as measured against the person's own attitudes, expectations, and personal desires before one concludes that he or she is called to the ministry.

A person's call to ministry occurs *within the body life of the church*. Thus, there is both an internal and an external verification of the call. The congregation serves as the external validating factor for a person's sense of call to the ministry. A person does not appoint him/herself to the ministry; one must be chosen by the church. By affirming the person's strengths and gifts, the congregation gives credence to an individual's call to ministry. The congregation affirms that the person is a member in good standing of the community of believers, and has demonstrated leadership capabilities.

Often the call is initiated by the congregation *before the person hears an inner call*. In such cases, the individual is responsible to respond to the discernment of the congregation. Congregations are called to be open to the Spirit's movement within their corporate life and faithful in calling out those whom God has gifted for ministry.

The conference and denomination validate the call by considering the relational integrity of the individual to the conference and denomination. What is the person's style of leadership? How does he or she come to terms with role expectations in ministry at the congregational and conference or denominational level without violating his/her conscience? A good style of leadership is to tend the flock of God, not under compulsion but willingly, not for sordid gain but eagerly, not domineering or lording it over those in your charge but by being an example (1 Peter 5).

Qualifications Relating to the Task or Function

It is the responsibility of both the church and the person called to ministry to match personal gifts with the task (specific task/function + particular gifts/talents/abilities = fruitful ministry). Following are some examples:

1. *Preacher/Teacher*: Obviously the gift of preaching and/or teaching is important here. The preacher has that special gift wherein the Word of God, by means of the Holy Spirit and grace, becomes known and shared through proclamation. The teacher is able to teach and train others while remaining teachable him/herself.

2. *Pastor/Shepherd*: In this area one demonstrates gifts such as: to offer care and nurture to others, to lead without dominating, to have empathy and an openly affirming attitude toward others.

3. *Administrator/Organizer*: Skills include organizational

planning, problem solving, delegation of authority, people motivation, and evaluation processing.

4. *Prophet/Evangelist*: A love for the world combined with bold and critical judgment about worldly values is needed here. Witness and outreach skills are imperative for this task, along with a heartfelt love for the lost and unrepentant.

Not every pastoral leader will have strengths in all of these areas, and some will need the assistance which shared leadership can provide. Often this supplemental, or shared, leadership is available from within the congregation. Larger congregations may be able to call several ministers with the requisite gifts available through a ministerial leadership team.

Educational Qualifications

It is preferable for a person to have professional training, experience, and/or formal education as preparation for most ordained ministry offices. A Master of Divinity degree is highly recommended and encouraged for those in pastoral ministry. Continuing education is expected.

The candidate for ministry will demonstrate an openness to learning and a general avoidance of rigidity. A basic understanding of biblical and theological studies is presumed, including a general knowledge of church history and doctrine. A clear grasp and understanding of Anabaptist-Mennonite identity, theology, and faith is assumed as well.

Finally, some roles or offices may require specialized training and education, such as counseling techniques for the pastor who specializes in pastoral counseling, or sociology/anthropology for one specializing in "inner-city" or "mission" work. There are many broad areas which can be narrowed down to a specialized focus for development, requiring specialized training, education, and experience. A basic general level of education and training at a Mennonite seminary is the foundation for such specialization.

Section V.
Ethics in Ministry

A. Introduction

Ethics for ministers, congregational leaders, and conference and denominational staff are based on the covenant relationship with God expressed in Jesus Christ, a covenant which is renewed at the Lord's Supper. This covenant is formed with Christ and the church at baptism, and is strengthened through every moment of grace experienced in the body of Christ.

Ethical standards are set to create and maintain loving, caring, responsible relationships within the church. The church recognizes the value of guidelines and principles for assisting in the development of ethics for congregational leaders, ministers, conference ministers (overseers/bishops), and administrators.

B. General Principles

1. Accountability Systems for Pastors

Persons in pastoral ministry develop multiple accountability relationships with elders/deacons, church chair and board, and the conference minister/overseer/bishop. (In some cultural settings, accountability may take a different form.) The Memo of Understanding addresses such matters as job description, the "review of ministry" planning process (which can be initiated by either pastor or elders/deacons), and regular settings for mutual feedback, nurture, reference, counsel, and support. Principles that guide both pastor and congregational leaders include: the health of the congregation, sensitivity to the minister's needs, and concern not to injure individuals or contribute to the failure of the ministry.

2. Accountability for Elders/Deacons/Lay Ministers

Congregational leaders have accountability systems within the congregation where they serve. Job descriptions provide clarity about responsibilities and duties. Regular reviews of their work provide feedback and accountability as well as support. Periodic meetings for fellowship and study with other persons charged with similar responsibilities are another form of accountability.

Successful litigation against elected congregational leaders and pastors has created awareness of the responsibilities of these offices and the need for clear accountability systems.

3. Accountability for Ministers in Denominational and Conference Offices

Persons called to these offices of the church are accountable to both the congregation in which they hold membership and to the conference which has granted the credential (see chart on p. 82). Conference ministers also are accountable to their peers in other conferences through regular gatherings which provide counsel and encouragement. All conference leaders must be accountable to a conference committee, which establishes written agreements defining what accountability means in their particular conference.

4. Accountability of Ministers to Conference

The minister respects the conference and denomination and assertively promotes conference and denominational concerns in the congregation. The minister is accountable to the area conference as well as to the congregation. Regular attendance at conference sessions and a local ministerial group is expected. The minister takes seriously the counsel of and supports the overseer and/or the conference minister and conference leadership.

5. Accountability Between Persons in Pastoral Ministry

The minister does not interfere in other people's ministry, whether in one's own congregation, other congregations, or other church institutions, unless authorized by appropriate bodies or invited to do so by all parties involved. The minister refrains from advocating on behalf of one party in a dispute and does not denigrate the integrity or ministry of other ministers, board members, or administrators who are called to ministry in that context.

Persons in pastoral ministry participate in regular, ongoing peer counseling (e.g., district ministerial group), including ecumenical pastoral settings. Caution and honesty are reflected in writing references for colleagues. Collegial support is given to other colleagues in times of personal, family, or congregational crisis and as a new colleague makes adjustments.

C. Use of Power

Persons in pastoral ministry need to recognize the temptation to exploit power. They seek to be authoritative rather than authoritarian. In times of conflict or controversy, the minister receives counsel from both within and outside the congregation to discern whether the issue belongs to the congregation or is a reflection on his/her leadership.

It is necessary to acknowledge one's own limitations as well as those of others. The minister avoids favoritism, participating in a clique, or building a group around him/herself. Persons in pastoral ministry refrain from cultivating a "lone ranger" style, but rather seek to enhance cooperation and interdependence with other leaders in the congregation. The stance is "our church" rather than "my church."

Persons in pastoral ministry model appropriate administrative behavior, passing on information, offering counsel and support, and maintaining a stance of care, accuracy, and competence. The minister trusts the congregation's decision-making ability and brings an appropriate theological perspective to that process. The role is that of both guide and facilitator.

Family Relationships

The minister seeks to maintain a healthy balance between church, spouse, and family. He/she models healthy differentiation of spouse and children from the pastor's role. The minister's spouse is encouraged to develop his/her own sense of identity, and to maintain clarity about this separate identity with the congregational leaders. Work demands are balanced with adequate spousal and family time.

Self-care

A minister's ability to provide pastoral care for others

is based on appropriate self-care. The minister informs congregational leadership when the balance between one's own needs and congregational expectations are getting out of balance. One's health must be nurtured by taking time for self, appropriate support and accountability systems, peer accountability, spiritual direction, counseling, and strong spousal and family relationships. While it is assumed that a minister will have a strong work ethic, it is also critical that a minister have a strong "rest ethic."

Accumulated crises can create great personal stress, and the minister should be aware of the value of seeking the support and/or counsel of a pastoral peer or conference minister. Realistic appraisal of one's own needs as well as written understandings about other support systems within the congregation can alleviate some of the stress. Competence in ministry and a healthful growing edge are maintained through continuing education courses and seminars.

Sexuality

Our deepest longings for God are related to our needs for intimacy with other human beings. Spiritual yearnings are related to our sexuality, which at times energize us for ministry. All ministers, whether serving within the congregation or a ministry outside the congregation, need to be clear about appropriate relationships.

Sometimes, however, relationships develop which are not appropriate. Because ministers are accorded authority and power in the church, such inappropriate relationships result in great pain and grief for the victim. It is imperative that the minister resist every temptation to develop such inappropriate relationships. Because of the power and authority implicit in the ministerial office, such inappropriate relating constitutes sexual harassment and abuse. The following more fully define sexual harassment or abuse (from *Guidelines for Discipline Regarding Ministerial Credentials*):

Unusual attention from a pastor, including such things as gifts, frequent social telephone calls, letters, private visits, and the maintenance of a special "spiritualized" partnership.

- Unsolicited or unwelcome flirtations, advances, or propositions.
- Sexual talk and innuendo.
- Graphic or degrading comments about another person's appearance, dress, anatomy.
- Display of sexually suggestive objects or pictures.
- Sexual jokes and offensive gestures.
- Sexual or intrusive questions about the person's personal life.
- Explicit descriptions of the minister's own sexual experiences.
- Abuse of familiarities or diminutives such as "honey," "baby," "dear."
- Unnecessary, unwanted physical contact such as touching, hugging, pinching, patting, kissing.
- Whistling, catcalls.
- Leering.
- Exposing genitalia.
- Physical or sexual assault.
- Sexual intercourse or rape.

To guard against self-delusion in such matters, ministers use referrals and consultations for support and counsel; ministers also acknowledge awareness of personal limitations, areas of temptation, and growing edges.

Celibacy is the standard for single persons and monogamous heterosexual relationships for married persons. Unmarried pastors guard against isolating themselves; they develop supportive relationships. Such relationships contribute to the social and spiritual well-being of the pastor. Courtship within the congregation one serves is discouraged.

Confidentiality and Truth-telling

Confidentiality requires vigilance. Disciplinary actions may be brought against a minister for violations of confidentiality. Pastors and elders/deacons develop understandings with each other around what is appropriately shared in an elders/deacons' meeting. When dealing with members who are ill or in the hospital, the pastor does not pass on patient information without permission from the patient; if the patient is unable to speak for him/herself, the family gives such permission.

All church leaders have a responsibility to model and coach others to speak the truth in love, avoiding the tendency to "triangle" others into one's concerns (telling a third party what one should rightly tell the person who has offended you). Elders/deacons encourage members to speak directly with the minister about concerns related to the minister, rather than speaking indirectly to the minister through the elders/deacons. In almost all cases, Jesus' instructions about going first to the brother or sister who has offended you (Mt. 18:15-20) are the basis for such truth-telling. A leader does not repeat the complaint to others on behalf of the person offended, but rather helps the person offended speak the truth for him/herself.

Similarly, conference ministers and administrators must have integrity in their consultations. Such integrity is found by honestly sharing information about hard-to-place pastoral ministry candidates, by sharing information with other conferences or denominations, and by forthrightness with ministerial candidates who are not suited to pastoral ministry.

In turn, the minister speaks the truth about him/herself, refraining from exaggeration or deception about credentials, training, experience, past record, finances, or convictions of crime or moral turpitude. The sharing of oneself wisely, to be known without shame as a redeemed child of God, breaks the destructive power of secrecy. One also has the right to refrain from speaking.

Impartiality

Persons in pastoral ministry seek to serve all persons from the congregation with impartiality, recognizing that one cannot pastor everyone.

Conference ministers and administrators with confidential personnel and placement information need to deal justly and impartially with all ministerial candidates and congregations. Whether in pastoral care or in working with the candidating process, one recognizes the temptations of rivalry and jealousy.

Leadership Style

Ministers maintain a leadership style that is gentle and

gracious but firm. Persons in pastoral ministry empower congregational members rather than seeking to be center stage. Differences will likely occur from time to time; nevertheless, it is expected that persons in pastoral ministry will speak well of the congregation and other congregational leaders where he/she serves.

Relationship of the Conference to the Pastor and Congregation

The conference provides the conference minister (or overseer) as a resource to pastors, their families, and congregational leaders. The conference minister (or overseer) provides counsel and shares leadership responsibilities in pastoral search and review processes, interim leadership, times of crisis, or conflict. However, in matters relating to ministerial credentials, final responsibility rests with the area conference to process all issues in granting credentials for ministry as well as disciplinary actions related to them.

It is the responsibility of the conference to establish guidelines regarding funerals, weddings, and other services by former pastors that will not undermine the role of the present pastor. As a rule, the congregation will sever ties with former pastors (see page 118).

D. For Persons in Pastoral Ministry

1. Oversight of the Candidate Process

The potential pastor takes the initiative to learn about the process that will be undertaken as he/she begins the candidate relationship. The candidate is careful to respect the congregation's process at each step. If a person who is not a member of the congregation's officially constituted search committee approaches the candidate, the candidate refers the inquiry to the search committee.

The pastoral candidate exercises confidentiality and care when seeking counsel. During the candidate process, the pastor may find it helpful to establish a confidential support group for him/herself.

2. **Preaching and Teaching**

The pastor faithfully interprets the Scriptures and avoids the temptation to overuse favorite themes. The pastor also refrains from "playing to the audience" and disciplines him/herself to engage biblical texts which are difficult or personally unattractive. Preaching supports, in a forthright manner, historic Anabaptist principles (e.g., pacifism, separation of church and state, believer's baptism, authority of Scriptures, the theology of the church as the covenanted body of Christ, etc.). Sermons are not self-righteous and do not manipulate guilt and shame.

Pastors are encouraged to exercise prophetic freedom. Both pastor and congregation seek a lifestyle consistent with the Sermon on the Mount. The pastor admonishes according to the teachings of Jesus in Matthew 18. Personal attacks from the pulpit demonstrate hostility and have no place in preaching. Plagiarism is dishonest, and the use of confidential material is a betrayal of trust. Overall, an attitude of respect for the congregation is apparent.

3. **In Pastoral Care and Counseling**

In pastoral care situations, the pastor has power that is derived from knowledge, experience, gender, social standing, body, role, office, and authority. Consequently, counseling is undertaken with great care for confidentiality, personal safety for the client and for the pastor, recognition of one's limitations, and the value of referral. The pastor closely monitors and controls his/her own fantasies and behavior. It is the responsibility of the pastor to maintain a relationship that is professional. Peer accountability and the use of referrals can support an appropriate professional relationship. Inappropriate sexual behavior in the counseling setting by the pastor is totally unacceptable; such behavior is a betrayal of trust, exploitative, abusive, has the overtone of incest, and may result in the counselee's suicidal behavior.

The pastor is encouraged to be familiar with the guidelines for counseling published by Canadian Association for Pastoral Education (CAPE), Clinical Pastoral Education (CPE), American Association for Marriage and Family Therapy (AAMFT), and with the *Guidelines for Discipline Regarding Ministerial Credentials*.

4. Relationship to Other Congregational Leaders

The pastor seeks a clear understanding of the congregation's mission, or assists the congregation to clarify or develop its mission, for it is on that foundation that the pastor works. The pastor models accountability for use of time, for working in a supportive, affirming, encouraging, conciliatory way, keeping leadership persons informed of and encouraging attendance at conference and church-wide events. The pastor reports to leaders regularly, seeking their counsel. In decision making and times of conflict, the best gifts the pastor can offer are an impartial, nonanxious presence and a theological framework for resolving the conflict.

5. **Relationship to the Community**

The pastor faithfully represents the congregation in the community. The congregation's theology guides its social action. The pastor acts as an advocate for ecumenical relationships and shapes the congregation's understandings of peacemaking, justice, and community. He/she seeks to enhance relationships among and between congregations, sharing resources in times of crisis and assisting the congregation's self-understanding as one part of the universal Christian church. Within the community, the pastor exercises responsibility in the maintenance of property/parsonage in keeping with congregational expectations and family needs. Personal appearance and lifestyle are congruent with simplicity and good stewardship and professionally appropriate to the congregation or conference where one serves. This includes financial responsibility to clear debts owed in the community prior to moving to another assignment.

6. **The Pastor and Stress Points**

During congregational conflict, the pastor, elders/deacons, and conference overseer seek outside assistance, preferably someone skilled in conflict management/resolution/mediation. Impartiality on the part of the pastor will increase the possibility of ongoing ministry in the congregation.

7. **Resignation and Leaving a Pastoral Assignment**

The pastor will process any decision around resignation or ending a pastoral assignment with the overseer/conference minister as well as the elders/deacons of the congregation prior to any public announcement. Together they will determine a clearly stated date of termination; such a date shall be set with respect for understandings between the pastor and congregation about the length of time to be given when "serving notice." The termination date will not be used as a threat or as leverage to stay longer. Both pastor and congregation are encouraged to plan a significant ending so both can move on to the next phase of life. Both seek to be realistic about how long it is possible to maintain interest following notice of termination. (For additional information, see also "Ministry Transition Packet" and "Congregational Information Packet" from the denominational department of ministerial leadership.)

8. **Ethics after Leaving a Ministerial Assignment**

The pastor whose assignment is finished usually does not remain in the congregation as a member, but seeks a new congregational home and exercises great sensitivity to his/her successor. The continuing reappearance of a former pastor at crisis points or life transition points interferes with the normal development of the relationships between the new pastor and members. Pastoral care is left in the hands of one's successor. Invitations to participate in weddings and funerals are declined. The best pastoral care offered by a former pastor is to attend the event rather than exercise public leadership. Return visits to the congregation are infrequent and casual.

In cases where it is impossible or unlikely that a pastor will be able to leave his/her congregation after the assignment is finished, an accountability group can be established to manage the "pastor emeritus" stage of ministry. This group carries responsibilities for tending to the relationship between the emeritus pastor and the congregation. The emeritus pastor is responsible to this group for his/her relating in the congregation and checks with this group about any requests that may come for ministerial duties. The new pastor and the overseer are part of this accountability group and give leadership to its functioning.

When other leaders leave their assignments, similar care should be taken to support the successor. When an elder/deacon or other congregational leader has held a position for many years, with authority and influence accruing during his/her tenure, care should be taken to disengage from this authority and influence in ways that are fair to the successor.

Similarly, conference ministers are encouraged to disengage from the conference in which they served and refrain from taking assignments in that conference which may frustrate the successor's attempts to minister. It is preferable for a conference minister to leave the conference for his/her next assignment. If that is not likely, it may be prudent for the conference to create an accountability group similar to the "pastor emeritus" group described above.

E. Ethics for Congregational Leaders

As leaders who share responsibility for guiding congregational life with the pastor and conference overseer, elders/deacons exercise great care to perform their responsibilities with integrity and sensitivity.

1. **Ethics in Calling a Pastor**

   Congregational leaders follow conference guidelines in calling a pastor. They work carefully through conference structures before contacting or calling a person who is pastoring another congregation in the same conference or elsewhere in the Mennonite church.

   The call to a pastor is extended, based on his/her credentials, without limitations based on gender, age, physical disabilities, or race. Persons who have experienced marriage failure and/or remarriage—or persons with other failures—are considered seriously as candidates only after a careful discernment process.

   Congregational leaders initiate honest conversations with the candidate about the process and how a call will finally be determined. A written job description and a written contract/covenant for the pastor is part of the calling process (see Section III). Congregational leadership maintains open communication with the pastor and will not allow a "party spirit" or gossiping to prevail. They will always work at facilitating a good relationship between candidate and the congregation.

2. **Preparing a Memo of Understanding (Covenant of Agreement)**

   a. Ministry Descriptions

      Clear, written expectations agreeable to both pastor and congregation should include the following: job description, time commitment, pastor's title, accountability, support structures, process for planning review and feedback, honoraria, availability during vacation, etc. Expectations are realistic, not excessive. This document is reviewed and revised periodically, to reflect changing expectations. Where the pastor serves full-time, ministerial activities outside the congregation occur with prior approval by congregational leadership.

Should differences arise, counsel is sought from the conference minister/overseer. Some congregations find it helpful to create a Pastor-Congregation Relations Committee (see #3 below), which is given the task of tending to the relationship between the pastor and the congregation. The PCRC is accountable to the administrative structure of the congregation (e.g., Church Council) in the event that additional counsel and processing is needed.

b. Salary

The salary paid to the pastor is commensurate with the pastor's training, experience, and responsibilities; the salary is also appropriate for the local cost of living. Salary is reviewed annually in consultation with the pastor. Some conferences (such as the Conference of Mennonites in Canada) publish yearly guidelines, as do Ministerial Leadership Services (GC) and the Mennonite Board of Congregational Ministries (MC).

c. Memo of Benefits

Benefits are those things in addition to cash

salary; they include such things as retirement benefits, partial and long-term disability insurance, medical benefits, family crisis leave, maternity leave, vacations, sabbatical, continuing education allowance, and book/periodicals allowance. Reimbursement for expenses incurred on behalf of the congregation are not considered benefits. Such reimbursement would include car allowance, meals hosted on behalf of the congregation, and expenses for attendance at area conference meetings, General Conference/General Assembly, etc.

d. Term of Service

In some traditions, the understood "term of service" is three or four years. In other traditions, the term of service is open-ended with no set length presumed. The Memo of Understanding (or Covenant of Agreement) should specify expectations.

e. Honoraria

The congregation provides written understanding regarding fees for services (honoraria) performed by the minister.

f. Part-time Employment

Where a pastor contracts for less than full-time employment, workload adjustments are appropriate. The pastor chooses a part-time vocation consistent with the congregation's beliefs, one which will not interfere with effective congregational service.

3. **Pastor-Congregation Relationships**

Larger congregations are encouraged to establish a

Pastor-Congregation Relations Committee; such a group is charged with tending to the relationship between the pastor and the congregation. Without such a committee, the elders/deacons are usually the minister's support and accountability group. In either case, the relationship is one of mutual counsel, support, and ongoing feedback. The attitude of congregational leaders who relate most closely to the pastor can make ministry a journey joyfully shared—or a wounding experience.

In a time of personal crisis (such as illness of a minister or family member, death in the family, psychological or emotional difficulties), the elders/deacons go the second mile, offering love, trust, and personal support for the minister and family, and adjusting his/her workload accordingly. The conference minister/overseer is notified (with the pastor's permission) to give additional counsel and support. Similarly, a review process can be a time of significant trauma for the minister. A congregational leader and the overseer provide pastoral care to the minister during this time.

4. **Relating to a New Pastor**

When a new minister enters a congregation, a new relationship is established with the elders/deacons. Congregational leaders focus carefully on the new relationship, avoiding behavior or activities that hinder the development of the new relationship. Accordingly, elders/deacons shape congregational behavior which permits the relationship with the previous minister to lapse. Specifically, this means declining invitations from congregational members to have the former minister officiate at weddings or funerals; the elders/deacons place all pastoral care dynamics firmly in the hands of the new minister. By providing such leadership, the elders/deacons will create an environment in which members of the congregation will more readily transfer their love and support to the new minister.

The pastor and elders/deacons will make an honest effort to understand and fulfill the responsibilities in the Memo of Understanding/ministry description and congregational job descriptions.

5. **Outside Requests**

Requests that fall outside the usual pastoral work should be reviewed jointly by the minister and elders/deacons; this includes requests from nonmembers for services such as funerals and weddings.

F. Ethical Guidelines for Other Situations

When Covenantal Relationships Are Broken

Unfortunately, there are times when a minister abuses the trust placed in him/her by the congregation. Sometimes such abuse severely damages the covenantal relationship between congregation, its leaders, and the minister.

In such situations, the area conference (through the congregation's overseer or conference minister) establishes a Ministerial Committee for Hearing and Review. The following examples are breaches of the trust by a minister which would justify a hearing and review process (for a detailed description, see *Guidelines for Discipline Regarding Ministerial Credentials*):

- Violations of confidentiality.
- The effort to subvert or to cause a congregation to withdraw from membership in conferences.
- Intentional deceptions and dishonesty, including misrepresentation of self in training or past records.
- Acts of physical or emotional violence.
- Gross neglect of ministerial responsibilities.
- Financial irresponsibility and irregularities.
- Major theological deviation from Christian and Anabaptist Mennonite understandings.
- Acts of sexual abuse, sexual violence, sexual harassment, and sexual deviance from Christian norms.
- Failure to respond in an acceptable manner to bodies responsible for granting and maintaining ministerial credentials.
- Acts within or against a congregation, or behavior which undermines service of another minister, all of which betray the trust granted the ministerial office.

Multiple-Staff Leadership and Special Assignments

Each minister in a multiple-staff congregation needs an individual job description and a memo of understanding which specifies the length of service. Sensitivity is exercised when negotiating job descriptions; this includes length of service, salary, and a memo of understanding for each minister. Team checkups with the conference minister/overseer or peer accountability groups can enhance team leadership and function; expectations need to be clarified periodically. Where women and men work together in ministry, sexuality can be an issue and should be addressed honestly and forthrightly.

Interim/Transition Ministry

Interim/Transition Ministers (see Glossary for a description of each) have full rights and responsibilities to provide ministerial leadership in the congregation. Congregations are encouraged to call seasoned Mennonite ministers for this role and are discouraged from calling ministers from other Christian denominations. While the call comes from the congregation, the interim minister may carry additional conference understanding about job description (of which the congregation is made fully aware) to work with one or more of the following:

- The congregation's conflict or pain.
- Grief, misunderstandings, feelings of loss, fear, anxiety, need for reconciliation.
- Seeking clarity about the congregation's mission.
- Developing strategies for increasing the health of the congregation.
- Clarifying the role and relationship of a pastor in the congregation.

Sensitivity and caution are exercised in making changes in the congregation's worship patterns and other areas as well.

The *interim/transition* minister does not campaign for a permanent assignment in the congregation. The elders/deacons, also, do not lead the congregation to call an interim/transition minister to a permanent assignment. The interim/transition minister offers the greatest service by giving unencumbered help and then moving on.

Chaplaincy, Noncongregational, or Special Assignment

Any person granted ministerial credentials for such assignment (chaplain, administrator of church institution, missionary) will be an active member of a Mennonite congregation. Each is accountable for his/her ministerial credentials to a review and accountability group established by the area conference. While such specialized ministers are responsible to their employers for job performance, they are accountable to the conference for the manner in which they treat the office and status of ministry bestowed on them by the conference through a ministerial credential. Accountability and discipline related to the ministerial credential follows the same procedures as those established by the conference for persons in pastoral ministry (see *Guidelines for Discipline Regarding Ministerial Credentials*). Congregations are encouraged to support such ministers by regularly inviting them to share the joys and concerns of their ministry and to consider such ministries as an extension of congregational life.

Glossary of Terms

Accountability. A relationship in which a minister voluntarily subjects his/her actions and ministry to a person or group that carries authority to represent the church.

Active. A category in the ordination credential designated for those with a charge for ministry.

Active Without Charge. A category in the ordination credential designated for those who do not have a ministerial charge; this credential is valid for no more than three consecutive years.

Aeltester. This is a German term which literally means "the oldest," and more to the point, "elder." It does not correspond, though, with most North American Mennonites' understanding of the term *elder*. It is closer to the term *bishop* or *overseer*, for it is an oversight ministry. In the "Kirchliche" Mennonite tradition, the Aeltester was the only one who could ordain, baptize, or serve communion. (It was also common for the Aeltester to have fairly wide authority in determining polity and/or settling disputes.) This was an elected office, and normally persons qualified, or were considered, only after significant experience in ministry. Once elected, a "second" ordination would take place.

Anti-clericalism. Opposition to the interference or influence of clergy in secular affairs (Webster). In this document, it also refers to a kind of negative reaction of laypeople to what was experienced as arid professionalism.

Apostolic Succession. The claim on the part of some communions that there is "an unbroken line of clerical ordination from the apostles to the present time." In the Anabaptist tradition, the notion of apostolic succession is lodged in the apostolic teachings (i.e., the Scriptures) and not the office.

Authority. The right, or the empowerment (conferred), to make certain decisions in a given area (jurisdictional, geographical, or philosophical). "Power to influence or command thought, opinion, or behavior" (Webster). Authority is conferred, earned, or taken; or it is built on some combination of those aspects.

Bench. "The term `bench' came to refer to the official ministerial body of the congregation including bishop, preachers, and deacons" (*Mennonite Encyclopedia*). The bench was a form of plural ministry and congregational leadership; members of the bench were all ordained. In this tradition, the bench was the governance group before the church council phenomenon secularized the process.

Bishop. An office emphasizing spiritual oversight of ministers (pastors) and often of congregations. The bishop in many cases is the equivalent of the German "Aeltester" (see above). Normally, in the Mennonite Church, a bishop was chosen from among a group of ministers, usually by lot. This was followed by a special ordination. There is no uniform description, however, that applies to all the Mennonite conferences or groups. In this document, the terms *bishop* and *overseer* are used to describe the same office.

Bi-vocational Minister. The term suggests that an ordained person has two vocations, one in ministry and another in some other field of work. A minister is always a minister, even if he/she spends some time on another job.

Call(ing). [1] The sense, or experience of, being urged/invited (by the Lord, first of all) to consider or enter some form of ministry. [2] The call of the congregation to a person to pursue ministry (thus an affirmation of the call as in #1), or the act of calling a person to serve as minister in a given place, who has already been affirmed and/or ordained.

Chaplaincy. One form of specialized ministry (usually by ordained individuals) in noncongregational settings, commonly in institutions such as schools, hospitals, prisons, retirement homes, etc.

Church. In this document, the term generally refers to the association of Mennonite congregations in North America who have covenanted together as a conference or denomination. The term *congregation* is normally used to refer to the group of believers organized and gathered in a local setting.

Commissioning. A form of recognition by the congregation, which usually does not carry a ministerial credential from the conference. In some parts of the church, however, congregations request that their conference recognize these persons with a credential.

Conference. A regional organization of Mennonite congregations, covenanting together for purposes of governance, mission, service, and fellowship;... a kind of subdivision of the denomination. In this document, the term also means "area conference."

Conference Minister. An oversight ministry at the conference level which involves being pastor to overseers and/or pastors as well as congregations. Linking pastors and congregations, arranging for mentors, organizing clusters of pastors, etc., are other significant duties associated with this office.

Confession of Faith. In a general way, this refers to the statement of beliefs to which an individual or group subscribes. The term may also denote or underline the claim that this is not a creed but a confession, thus more in line with Anabaptist understandings. The current confession of faith is entitled *Confession of Faith in a Mennonite Perspective*.

Congregation. The local community of believers in a specific place, covenanted together for worship, fellowship, and mission.

Congregational Autonomy. The understanding that all decision-making power rests in the congregation.

Convergence. A moving closer together, or even a move toward agreement on issues, polity, or beliefs by two or more bodies. The movement may begin independently rather than by deliberate action.

Covenant. In simple terms, an agreement. In religious life, it acquires more significance because it is usually understood as an agreement built on promises made in the presence of God. In this context, one thinks of the relationships between pastor and congregation, between the congregation and the conference, and between each conference and the denomination as *covenantal*.

Credential. The testimonial (perhaps a certificate) that shows a person has the right, or is entitled, to hold, or exercise, a certain [ministry] position or office.

Deacon. Traditionally, those who served the poor and needy and visited the sick. They were ordained for life and formed part of the threefold ministry. Today, in addition to the above, deacons often serve as support to the pastor and are involved in planning the spiritual ministry of the congregation. Some are involved in worship leading, preaching, counseling, conflict resolution, discipline, etc. In this regard, the office is quite similar to the congregational *elder*. The term *deacon* includes both men and women, although some congregations and conferences prefer the term *deaconess* when referring to women. Currently, this is a term position in most congregations.

Deaconess. This office has a special history, with some roots in the Lutheran tradition. Among Mennonites in Kansas, there was an order called the Bethel Deaconesses: women dedicated to caring for the sick. See also *deacon*.

Denomination. The larger organization of a particular Christian tradition, in this case encompassing various conferences and congregations. In this document, the term usually applies to the Mennonites in North America.

Department of Ministerial Leadership. A term used in this document to denote a denominational office(s) with responsibility to provide coordination and resources for area conferences. This includes administration and pastoral care for conference personnel concerned with ministerial leadership.

Discipline. To censure or reprimand for the purpose of correction, usually understood to be done by an official body such as a board, commission, or perhaps congregation.

Elder. In the General Conference (U.S.), this is the term that came to be used for the person ordained to "full-service ministry," meaning that they could baptize, serve communion, and ordain. In the General Conference (Canada), the term (usually in German *Aeltester*) retained more the meaning of oversight, similar in role and function to the bishop. In the Mennonite Church, the term is currently used to describe a ministry of lay leadership in congregational life; elders assist the pastoral leader(s) and have limited terms of office. In this document, the term is used to describe the role of congregational leaders other than the pastor (deacons, lay ministers).

Endorsement. Affirmation, sanction, or approval, usually of a person, for a particular task or office. It implies backing, and a kind of giving of authority. An example would be where a denomination gives its affirmation to someone who will be serving in a wider ecumenical or public setting (e.g., hospital or prison chaplaincy).

Evaluations/Reviews. A process designed to assess the performance/suitability of a person in a particular office, which includes both affirmation and constructive advice for the purpose of growth and improvement.

File/Profile. The dossier of a person in ministry, which minimally includes a completed *Ministerial Leadership Information Form*, along with a composite of references.

It may include other supplementary data, e.g., resumes, ordination documents, etc.

General Assembly. The biennial gathering of delegates from the twenty-one conferences in the Mennonite Church to do the business of the denomination. Before 1971, this gathering was called "Mennonite General Conference."

General Conference Mennonite Church. The name of a Mennonite conference begun in 1860, which today includes many congregations in Canada, the United States, and Latin America. The individual congregations send delegates to triennial General Conference sessions, and the central office is in Newton, Kansas.

Inactive. A category in the ordination credential designated for those who have been without a charge for more than three consecutive years or have left the denomination. This credential is not valid for performing any ministerial functions.

Interim Minister. The person who takes a short-term assignment in ministry in a congregation, between the end of a longer term pastor and the beginning of another, to maintain basic ministry (see page 126). Sometimes this person is referred to as a **Transition Minister.** As above, but with a more specific assignment that includes healing, reconciliation, and setting new sights or directions.

Lay Ministry. Ministry usually done *gratis*, commonly by people without formal training, on a marginal-time basis. Lay ministers may have been ordained in the past but more commonly now are commissioned by the congregation. They normally make their living at another occupation or take a kind of "tent-making" approach.

Licensing. A credential for ministry which can be granted for two reasons: for a ministry limited in time, position, role, or geographical location. A second reason for granting a license relates to ordination. In this case, a two-year license is granted to ministers who are anticipating ordination; this two-year period provides opportunity to discern the minister's gifts, abilities, and aptitude.

Lot, the. The pattern of selecting leaders in the church by drawing the lot (usually a slip of paper placed in one of several Bibles). This is a nonelection method. Members usually have a say in nominating individuals, but congregations which use this process understand the choice to be in God's hands.

Mennonite Church. The name of that group of area conferences in North America and Puerto Rico which choose to have membership in and send delegates to a biennial General Assembly. Offices are located in Elkhart County, Indiana, and Scottdale, Pennsylvania. Also known earlier as the "Old Mennonites."

Mennonite General Conference. Not to be confused with the General Conference Mennonite Church, this refers to the gathering of area conference delegates in the "Old Mennonite" Church before its reorganization in 1971. This gathering is now called "General Assembly."

Mentoring. The practice of walking beside, giving support and advice, by one experienced in ministry to someone new to the ministry.

Minister/Ministry. The service to which the whole people of God are called is ministry. This document acknowledges a double meaning for the term and focuses primarily on one of those meanings, specifically to the particular offices or forms of leadership in the church. It is a fairly broad or general term that does not define function.

Ministerial Leadership Information Form. The instrument used by the ministerial calling system of the General Conference Mennonite Church (Ministerial Leadership Services) and the Mennonite Church Board of Congregational Ministries (Ministerial Information Center) to gather personal, academic, and theological information about a candidate.

Ministry in Specialized Settings. Ministry performed in noncongregational settings, commonly in institutions such as schools, hospitals, prisons, retirement homes, etc. This ministry is usually performed by ordained persons.

Multiple Staff. Two or more ministers serving one congregation and forming some kind of a unit or team. Sometimes deacons/elders and musicians/choir leaders are considered part of a multiple-staff unit.

Office(s) of Ministries. The term usually describes a position that is recognized for the purpose of exercising authority or some ministerial functions. It can be filled or vacant. Thus, one can speak of ministry as an *office*; as such, it belongs to the church.

Ordinal. A document containing instructions for the ordination of ministers. The term dates back to the fourteenth century. It was used as the name for such a document for the General Conference Mennonite Church in 1987.

Ordination. "Ordination is an approval for ministry, given by the church to women and men who have been called by God and the church to positions of leadership and ministry as a long-term commitment" (Ordinal, p. 19). The Waterford (1986) statement reads: "Ordination is an act by which the church, after appropriate personal and corporate discernment, calls and appoints a member to a particular ongoing leadership ministry in the life and mission of the church." Usually ordination also carries the added elements of consecration/dedication [covenant making] and granting credentials.

Overseer. In the Mennonite Church, this is a pastor or conference leader who provides oversight to congregations and pastors. Some Mennonite Church conferences have moved from the bishop model to the overseer model. Overseers are usually discerned and appointed by congregations, pastors, and conference leadership commissions. They usually serve for a specific term. There are variations from conference to conference in the practical details of this office and its ministry.

Pastor. A term commonly used to designate the spiritual leader of the congregation. In this document, it is more often used to describe a "shepherding" function of a minister (i.e., *pastoral ministry*).

Plural Ministry. Another term for multiple staff, though not necessarily implying that all are paid. This refers to a group that shares the ministerial leadership tasks.

Polity. "The form of government of a religious denomination" (Webster). In common usage, this is expanded to include policies, understandings, and practices of the denomination.

Preacher/*Prediger*. A term commonly used in the past by both General Conference and the Mennonite Church traditions for the spiritual leaders of the congregation.

Probation. A category in the ordination credential designated for those whose ministry has been placed under close supervision by the conference for a specified period of time in order to determine whether the ministerial credential should be continued.

Progression of Ordination. Some parts of the Mennonite tradition practice a second ordination to the office of bishop. This included a second rite, separate from the ceremony ordaining the person to ministry.

Retired. A category in the ordination credential designated for those who retire from active ministry and are at least fifty-five years of age.

Sacramentalism. The belief that there is some power or grace contained in a rite, or ceremony, itself. For example, that something extra is received by the person ordained by virtue of the rite of ordination.

Specialized Ministries. See Ministry in Specialized Settings.

Suspended. A category in the ordination credential designated for those whose ministerial credential has been laid aside temporarily for reasons of ethical misconduct. Such a credential is not valid for performing ministerial functions.

Terminated. A category in the ordination credential designated for those whose ministerial credential and ordination have been rescinded. This is a permanent action; such a credential is not valid for the performance of any ministerial functions.

Threefold Ministry. This refers to the traditional pattern of bishops, pastors, and deacons/elders. This document describes a governance structure for Mennonite congregations incorporating these three offices. The three offices are delineated as those having oversight (conference ministers, overseers or bishops), those providing daily practical ministry (pastors, chaplains, pastoral counselors, evangelists, missionaries), and those in shared but nonprofessional leadership roles (deacons, elders, or lay preachers).

Transfer. Moving of credentials of a minister from one conference to another.

Validating. The testing and approving of persons being considered for licensing, commissioning, or ordination (see Vesting/Lodging).

Vesting/Lodging. The granting and maintaining/keeping of credentials. This assumes a responsible body authorized to grant, review, monitor, and withdraw credentials.

Sources Consulted

Abba, R. *The Interpreter's Dictionary of the Bible*. New York: Abingdon Press, 1962. Volume III—"Priests and Levites."

"Additional Awareness," Centre for the Prevention of Sexual and Domestic Violence, 1914 North 34th St., Suite 105, Seattle, WA 98103-9058, $.50 U.S.

AMBS Ministry Statement, Fifth Draft (51188), Elkhart, Ind.

Baptism, Eucharist and Ministry, Faith and Order Paper No. 111, World Council of Churches, Geneva, Switzerland, 1982.

Barrett, C. K. Church, *Ministry and Sacraments in the New Testament*. Grand Rapids, Mich.: William B. Eerdman Publishing Company, 1985.

Bauman, Harold. *Congregations and Their Servant Leaders*. Scottdale, Pa.: Herald Press, 1982.

Bender, Ross Thomas. *The People of God*. Scottdale, Pa.: Herald Press, 1971.

Carroll, Jackson. *As One with Authority*. Louisville, Ky.: Westminster/John Knox Press, 1991.

Church Leadership and Ordination: Study Guide for Congregations, Committee on the Ministry, General Conference Mennonite Church, 1972.

Confession of Faith in a Mennonite Perspective, Scottdale, Pa.: Herald Press, 1995.

Ellis, E. Earle. *Pauline Theology: Ministry and Society*. Grand Rapids, Mich.: William B. Eerdman Publishing Company, 1989.

Fung, Ronald Y. K. *Evangelical Review of Theology*, April, 1984. Volume 8, No. 1—"Function or Office? A Survey of the New Testament Evidence."

Fung, Ronald Y. K. *The Evangelical Quarterly*, 1980. Volume 52, No. 4—"Charismatic Versus Organized Ministry? An Examination of an Alleged Antithesis."

Giles, Kevin. *Patterns of Ministry Among the First Christians*. CollinsDove, North Blackburn, 1989.

Grumm, Meinert. *Currents in Theology and Mission*, 1989. Volume 16—"Ministry: The Old Testament Background."

Guidelines for Counseling, AAMFT and CAPE, American Association for Marriage and Family Therapy, 1100 17th St. NW, 10th floor, Washington, DC 20036. Canadian Association for Pastoral Education, P.O. Box 96, Roxboro, Quebec H8Y 3E8.

Guidelines for Discipline Regarding Ministerial Credentials, Ministerial Leadership Services (GC), Newton, Kans., and Mennonite Board of Congregational Ministries (MC), Elkhart, Ind., 1993.

Harder, Helmut. *Accountability in the Church: A Study Guide for Congregations*, Conference of Mennonites in Canada, Winnipeg, 1985.

Klaassen, Walter. *Anabaptism in Outline*. Scottdale, Pa., and Kitchener, Ont.: Herald Press, 1981.

Krahn, Cornelius. *Dutch Anabaptism*. Scottdale, Pa.: Herald Press, 1981.

Leadership and Authority in the Life of the Church. A Summary Statement, Mennonite Church General Assembly, 1981.

Lebold, Ralph. *Learning and Growing in Ministry*. Scottdale, Pa.: Herald Press, 1986.

Loewen, Howard John. *One Lord, One Church, One Hope and One God: Mennonite Confessions of Faith*, Institute of Mennonite Studies, Elkhart, Ind., 1985.

Mennonite Confession of Faith, Scottdale, Pa., and Kitchener, Ont.: Herald Press, 1963.

Mennonite Encyclopedia, Dyck, Cornelius J. and Martin, Dennis D., eds. Scottdale, Pa., and Waterloo, Ont.: Herald Press, 1990. Articles consulted:
    Vol. V – Authority
           – Bishop
           – Elder
           – Ordination
           – Pastoral Education
           – Polity
           – Priesthood of All Believers

Mennonite Encyclopedia, Krahn, Cornelius, Gingerich, Melvin, and Harms, Orlando, eds. Scottdale, Pa.: Mennonite Publishing House; Newton, Kans.: Mennonite Publication Office; Hillsboro, Kans.: Mennonite Brethren Publishing House, 1957. Articles consulted:

    Vol. I – Bishop
    Vol. II – Deacon

     – Deaconess
     – Elder
  Vol. III – Lot
     – Ministry
     – Ministry, Call to the
  Vol. IV – Ordination
     – Preacher

Miller, Paul M. *Servant of God's Servants*. Scottdale, Pa.: Herald Press, 1967.

Minister's Manual, Janzen, Heinz and Dorothea, eds. Newton, Kans.: Faith and Life Press, 1983.

Mosemann, John H. *Ordination, Licensing and Installation*. Newton, Kans.: Faith and Life Press, 1983. Worship Series No. 13.

Ordinal: Ministry and Ordination in the General Conference Mennonite Church, Ministerial Leadership Services, Newton, Kans., 1987.

Pastor-growing—People-growing, Mennonite Board of Education (Pastorate Project), 1995.

Proceedings from the 1984 (Stryker, Ohio) and the 1986 (Waterford, Ind.) consultations, sponsored by the Mennonite Board of Congregational Ministries (MBCM).

Sauder, Renee. Women in Pastoral Ministry Survey, Mennonite Board of Congregational Ministries, Elkhart, Ind. (unpublished), 1993.

Sawatsky, Rodney. *Authority and Identity: The Dynamics of the General Conference Mennonite Church*, Bethel College, North Newton, Kans., 1987.

The Believers Church: Proceedings of the Study Conference, General Conference Mennonite Church, Newton, Kans., 1955.

The Minister's Manual, General Conference Mennonite Church, 1950.

Wenger, John C. *The Complete Writings of Menno Simons*. Scottdale, Pa.: Herald Press, 1956.

Zook, Gordon. Surveys of Pastoral Leadership Models in the Mennonite Church, Mennonite Board of Congregational Ministries, Elkhart, Ind. (unpublished), 1982 and 1985.

Index